Born Out Of Season

By: MARSHAL RALPH L. HOOKER

REBEL PUBLISHING COMPANY, INC.

TEXARKANA, TEXAS

First Printing - October 1981
Second Printing - November 1988
Third Printing - March 1993

©1981 by Rebel Publishing Company, Inc., Rt. 5 Box 347-M, Texarkana, Texas 75501. All rights reserved. Printed in the United States of America by Southwest Printers and Publishers, Inc., Texarkana, Arkansas.

**Library of Congress Catalog Card Number 81-84090
International Standard Book Number 0-9605666-1-9**

This little book has been a long winter of remembering for me — happy remembering and sad remembering, exciting and dull. I owe many thanks to my sweet wife, Katy, who put up with all my silences and typed the rough draft; to my good friend, Lennea Nikkel, who put it in order for publication; and to Oran Scurlock, the publisher, who encouraged and prodded me to get these thoughts down on paper.

Ralph L. Hooker

Preface

Dear readers of this little book:

My writing this book is not meant to imply that I was a great and brave person, and certainly not to make anyone's misdeeds seem anything but wrongdoing. I offer no excuse for any of my wrongs; some were the growing pains of a young person, the influence of older persons, and the times and circumstances, including the depression days when I stole to eat and exist. All of that I am not proud of. I have only contempt for anyone who takes that which is not his, which someone else has earned by hard labor. This may be exciting at the time, but there is always that payday.

I can't expect anyone to understand my thinking and reasoning on some of these things, but remember you were not there; and I mostly did what seemed the thing to do at the time. It is true I rode horseback with outlaws in Oklahoma, with a price on my head. Also, it is true that in later life I paid back everyone I had wronged when I could find them. Some broke down in tears, and no one called the law on me. Some who had died, moved, or disappeared I couldn't find. I had a detective try to locate them, and when I couldn't find them, I put the money in a church.

Anyone doing wrong will find "The way of the transgressor is hard." * It may yield profit and excitement at the time, but never happiness and satisfaction — and there is always that awful payday! For "the wicked shall not go unpunished." § If you build something and it is unsatisfactory, or take a wrong road, or say the wrong thing, you can start again and do it right. But if you live a wrong life and die that way, you just won't make it! Be honest with yourself. If you have hurt people, taken what isn't yours, been untruthful, abused your body — the one body which God has given you — or transgressed in any way, you had better change while there is time.

Christ said, "For I have left you an example that you should do as I have done." + If Christ wouldn't do it, you better not. It is easy when you are young, and seem to have lots of time ahead, to disregard any warning, but we don't have assurance of life for even the next few minutes. Some let the scorn of friends influence them wrongly. We won't care at all what our friends think when we are facing GOD and our past life. Even so, that time comes all too soon.

Enough of preaching. It is only that I have been there, and I know what it means to be sorry. I would leave this one thought with you: God doesn't want us to be sick, sad, or in any kind of trouble, but to enjoy life and health, and many years of prosperity and happiness in HIS way. "AND YOU SHALL LOVE THE LORD YOUR GOD WITH ALL YOUR HEART, AND WITH ALL YOUR SOUL, AND WITH ALL YOUR MIGHT," and Him only shall you serve.

RALPH L. HOOKER
the old marshal

---

*Proverbs 13:15
§Proverbs 11:21
+John 13:15
−Deuteronomy 6:5

Contents

Chapter I	1
Chapter II	6
Chapter III	11
Chapter IV	15
Chapter V	21
Chapter VI	28
Chapter VII	33
Chapter VIII	39
Chapter IX	49
Chapter X	64
Chapter XI	71
Chapter XII	78
Chapter XIII	89
Epilogue	100

Chapter I

WELL, there I was, my first day on earth, June 13, 1906, at 1247 James Street in Carthage, Missouri. I didn't know it then, and wasn't much interested, but it was the beginning of a fairly long life — an interesting life, and one that would be no stranger to sorrow, grief, and hardship. But I had my good times, too.

My father, Daniel E. Hooker, was employed at the time laying "Carthage Stone" sidewalks in the town, using stone from the largest limestone quarry in the world, located right there at Carthage. He later worked for the old Kellog Marble Works as a stone cutter, and in later years had his own business. Father had three brothers, Renzy, Bob, and Fate, and four sisters, Cora, Mary, May, and Cary, who were all living at 1234 James Street.

Joe Hooker, my father's father, came from Bedford County, Tennessee, on Duck River. When grandfather left Tennessee, he just got up from the table, went outside, and kept going. The family never knew where he went until in the 1960's. (On one of my trips, I went to Bedford County and told the relatives still living there that their missing brother and uncle was my grandfather.) Grandfather settled first on the Sarcoxie Prairie, where only one other white man was living then. My grandfather bought from this man a solid walnut cord bed. From Sarcoxie, he moved to Carthage, then to Pierce City, where he was one of the founding fathers of that town.

Grandfather was a store keeper; he had been running a store beside his home, but he never became wealthy for he gave too much credit to his nonpaying friends. He was also a minister, one of the group who started the Church of God in Carthage. During the Civil War, grandfather contracted tuberculosis, but he lived until 1903. His wife, my father's mother, was a Biddlecome. Grandma would tell how (during the Civil War) they would go out at night and knock wild turkeys out of the trees to get something to eat — afraid to fire a gun for fear of the bush whackers. They trapped prairie chickens, quail, and rabbits. Mother's people, originally from North Carolina, had a hard life, but their strong Christian faith sustained them.

Other Hookers came to Missouri. I knew only Uncle Ty. There was a brother, Bert, who lived in Wentworth, Missouri and ran a barber shop; he took his own life. John moved to Colorado; a tree fell on him and killed him.

1

Two sisters, Frances and Ava, stayed in Missouri.

Uncle Ty was quite a man, never married, and he could play a fiddle and violin like very few could. He made brooms in a box car workshop, and sold them, delivering them in a Model A Ford. He was a real hunter and also worked in the mines (good mines which put Wentworth on the map as long as the mines held out.) Uncle Ty had a pet skunk and hunting dogs. He always had a fine garden with wonderful watermelons. When he was an old man his house burned, the weather was bad, and he took pneumonia and died. He was buried in the Black Fox Cemetery southwest of Wentworth.

My father had an old bicycle, before they had coaster brakes, which he rode to work. Uncle Fate was riding one like that one day, going real fast down 13th street. A man crossed in front of him with a horse and a hack. The bicycle had no brakes, so Uncle Fate just stuck out his legs and crashed into the side of the horse. The collision nearly killed him and the horse, and did wreck the bicycle.

Times were hard and most people who could, kept a milk cow. One morning they went out to milk and the cow chased them out of the barn. They went up into the haymow and looked down on her — she tried to climb the walls to get them. The veterinarian said she had rabies and they had to shoot their cow.

One day a bunch of the kids were playing ball in the pasture by the house; the catcher missed the ball and it hit Uncle Fate in the forehead and both his eyes popped out. He had a real fit, so the boys all piled on him and held him down while one of them pushed his eyes back in.

Father and his brothers and sisters grew up on the outskirts of Carthage. They had exciting times like all kids while growing up.

As a little girl, my mother, Louie Page, lived in River Sioux, Iowa — sometimes called Little Sioux. Her father, Scott Page, would take them in boats on the old Missouri River. They left Iowa in a covered wagon and went to Gainesville, Texas. Besides his wife, Emma, there were Scott, Jr., Bertha, the older daughter, Ralph, for whom I was named, and my mother, Louie. After living in Texas awhile, Grandfather Page thought his boys might be taking up with the outlaws in the area, so he left and got into Oklahoma territory in time to take up Indian land in the run from Guthrie, Oklahoma.

Grandfather Page and Uncle Scott took their land joining each other nine miles southwest of Oklahoma City, which then was a small cow town. Uncle Scott rode a gray gelding he told me was almost tireless. While riding for a location, he scared up a deer, shot it with his Winchester, cut off its head and tied it to his saddle. Later he had that head mounted, and his son Russell has it in his home now. I had a picture of Uncle Scott and Uncle Ralph, taken at this time, with their pioneer clothes on and their Colt revolvers, which I valued very much, but an unscrupulous individual stole it for spite.

Mother told me that when they woke up the first morning on their new land, a large buck deer, a doe, and a fawn were looking at them from the willows lining each side of the little creek that ran through their place. The sun was just coming up and it was a beautiful sight. Also the prairie was covered white with bleached buffalo bones as far as you could see.

Grandmother Page was born a Denney, and her mother was a Sakket from Pennsylvania. I never knew much about Grandpa Page's people. I do know that he was in San Francisco during the earthquake in 1906, the year I was born. Uncle Ralph went to Alaska and struck it rich. He wrote to his family that he was going to Old Mexico to buy a ranch, and would come and get them. They never heard from him again.

South of 13th Street where I was born was all open, free range pasture. But father wanted to be out away from the town. We moved to what is now Buena Vista Road, then a bushy five acres with a creek in the middle. I was old enough by then to remember the spring floods. The water would get up into the house at times. Chickens, ducks, and all their paraphernalia would float off down stream somewhere. I loved to go upstream and jump into the water and let it carry me sailing down to the house, then I would swim out and do it some more. My Grandma Page owned this place. Father bought a place, all brush and up on higher ground, adjoining this one. He had his house almost finished and a bad storm came up and flattened it out, so he had to rebuild it. At this home I spent some of my happiest days. There was always lots of work to be done, but I had plenty of time to play, too. East of us was a huge pasture, lots of timber and tangled brush, real wild. Here was where I spent all the time I could.

My father, a fine stonecutter, cut a stone hitching post with a snake about to strike a dove. He traded that post for a large black and white collie dog, owned by a Mr. Oliver, who was moving to town and wanted to find a country home for his dog. This was the smartest, almost human, dog I ever knew and he was a really good guard dog. He would catch a rabbit so quickly

Old Tip. "Dad cut a stone hitchpost for a Mr. Oliver to get him. Best varmint, watch and companion dog that ever lived."

it was fantastic. If a crow or hawk would fly over our land, he would run under it until it was beyond our property. These were glorious times for a young boy out where there was so much small game. We kept a milk cow in this huge pasture, and the collie dog, Tip, would go get our cow out from a large herd and bring her in for milking.

There were several farm dogs that would seem to know when Saturday was, after I started to school. They would come at night and sleep on the porch; I would wake up and speak each one's name, and could tell how many were there when they would wag their tails and thump on the floor. They knew we would all get up early and spend a whole day hunting. We had plenty of rabbits to eat. Shortly after we got Tip, he treed a man in the chicken house. It was a little old bachelor who had rented my grandmother's house after we moved out. After that, I couldn't like him, and would slip out at night and throw rocks with a slingshot down on his tin roof. It sure did make him mad! We had a big rain and the creek was up really big. We boys went down to where he crossed the creek on a plank; we swam out and sawed the plank almost through, then turned it over. He came home after dark with his week's supply of groceries in his arms, the plank gave way, and he lost all his armload of groceries and nearly drowned. He moved shortly after that.

I was still small when Dad bought a 410 shotgun. I slipped it out and went hunting — I had to rest the barrel on something to hold it up — and shot my first rabbit. After that I managed to get a Hamilton 22 and a Quackenbush 22. I hid these under the bridge so my father wouldn't take them away from me. After my parents found out I had them and was shooting game for the neighbors, they let me keep them and also the game. There were some old mines south of us and the doves would light on the chat piles to get grit. I would sit in the brush and pick them off one at a time until we got enough for a meal. These rifles I had usually sold for $1.50, or for selling Cloverine Salve, and 22 shorts were 7¢ a box. Hunting was good, with plenty of game everywhere. I hunted all I could whenever the chance presented itself, and in the winter the porch was always lined with dressed game, frozen, and tacked up with nails.

I had a lot of fun hunting, and I liked to have my dog and rifle with me and go by myself. There was an empty house with this old farm I used as my hunting ground. It was the old Tangner place, and besides the house, it had an old race track and barns. Rabbits were thick all over the place, but they would run only a short distance and duck under the house in a small hole before my dog could catch them. I stopped up all the lesser holes and put a glass over the main one; the rabbits would run full blast into the glass and knock themselves out. All we had to do was pick them up.

The Frisco Railroad ran east of this place, and I hunted in the back part in quite dense brush. Many hoboes were on the train in those days. One day a man jumped out of the brush and tried to catch me. My dog was off hunting and couldn't help me. I was too small to outrun the guy. Boy! was I scared! When I saw I was going to lose the race I stopped and put the 410 on him. He came to a sudden halt, and went as fast as he could back to wherever he came from.

On Saturdays the colored boys would go jackrabbit hunting with their greyhounds. They would come by our place and get the dogs to fighting. Darrel Marcey brought out a large bulldog one day and set it on Tip. It was a real fight, and I was too small to stop it; I was afraid his bulldog would kill ours. That bulldog kept trying to get a throat hold, or a front leg, but our collie was too smart for him. He kept moving and slashing until he had the bulldog cut to pieces, so Darrel took his sad dog and left. Lots of nights we would be kept awake by the wolves fighting our dog in the yard, or on the porch.

I was doing chores for a Mrs. Wieland at a place north of our home, and her neighbor, Wilkerson had a mean white bulldog. I went up to do the chores for the old lady, and this dog ran me up a hackberry tree. I didn't have my dog along, so there was nothing to do but climb. I had a 1000 shot BB gun with me, and the dog wouldn't let me down, so I commenced to shoot. The tree was small, and he would jump up and try to grab me; I shot his eyes out, and his tongue was big and bleeding. Finally he left, and I did my chores and went home. That dog died, and old Mr. Wilkerson sure had fits about it!

The family just north of us, Mayfields, had a sorghum mill and I always helped them make sorghum in the fall. Old Grandpa Porter also made some really good sorghum — I had plenty of work helping them all. I loved to take care of our chickens and when I could I would get two old roosters to fighting. I got in wood and kindling, carried water up the hill in gallon buckets from our well. My father rode his bicycle to work and I would drive the buggy or whatever (I was so small I had to stand on the manger to put the breast strap or back band on to get hitched up) to town on Saturday afternoon to bring him and his bicycle home, and stop at Emerson's Grocery on the corner of Macon and Grand. Mr. Emerson always gave us a little candy when Dad paid his week's grocery bill. Life was good.

Chapter II

WHEN my first morning of school came I sure was upset! I was only a bashful country boy and all I wanted to do, besides the work I had to do, was get my dog and gun and head for the "boondocks." My! how I loved to spend days alone, except for my dog and gun, away out in the quiet woods. I only disliked school because it interfered with my plans. My first grade teacher was Lina Bell Nickles, and she was a very fine person. (My father's first teacher was Sally Boone — related to Daniel?) Our classes were held in the old three story red brick Washington School in what was Logston Hollow. We had a long way to walk and carried our lunch in a half gallon syrup bucket with our initials punched in the lid with a nail. We had real clean, nourishing food then, and plenty of it. No junk food in those days. Sometimes the snow was very deep and it was bitter cold; Mother would wrap us up good and tie gunny sacks around our legs. We nearly froze sometimes! We went from nine to four, and I only missed one day when the drifts were so deep I had to go back home. School was easy for me except arithmetic, and history was easiest. It is queer how some things stay in one's memory.

The neighbor boy, Lawrence Porter, who went to school with us, was three days older than I, and as we grew up we were good friends. His parents were good Christians like mine, but we boys had our differences. Lawrence and I had many fights, but we nearly always made up again.

We had plenty of horses; my favorite was a fine little buckskin mare, Dolly. She had a colt every year from a fine stallion, Captain Jupiter. The colts were allowed to run beside the buggy when we went to town. Then when we weaned them and shut them up, Dolly would give us a hard time. Many times she would be grazing and hear her colt nicker; she would go right through the fences to the barn. Then I had a job soaking her wire cuts in water from boiled mullen. Dolly was a branded western bronc, shipped in from Parsons, Kansas. She liked me and would let me ride her. I would pull her head down and straddle her neck; she would raise and slide me down onto her back. I would stretch way down and flank her with my toe; she'd lay her ears back and squeal, and pitch me over her head! Then we would do it all over again. I think she enjoyed this as much as I did. (I always looked for a soft place for this fun.)

There were a lot of cattle driven here and there, but no big trail drives in our area. Many gypsy wagon trains came through, stayed and traded livestock and picked up what they could. Mother warned me not to go near their encampments, but I just had to go see their horses.

There was a lot of work to be done. We tried to raise as much as we could to eat — all kinds of fruits and vegetables. Many of them went into the root cellar — apples, potatoes, carrots, etc.; and there were rows and rows of canned fruit and berries. We also dried lots of corn in sacks and hung it up. Did I ever hate to hoe all day out in the hot sun on that rocky hill! We didn't have much money — only one pair of shoes per child per year — but we ate well. I never saw bakery bread; we had homemade bread, biscuits, and corn bread. I kept wild game supplied most of the time for breakfast (fried rabbit), or we had pork, gravy, biscuits, fried potatoes, and any kind of fruit or berries.

We always butchered hogs in the late fall. Everyone pitched in and did their share. I would take the bladder and blow it up with air, and then when it dried it was a light ball to play with — about the size of a volleyball. The fresh meat on butchering day was sure fine, and I went for the liver. Our old collie dog would lie under the carcass we left hanging out to cool during the night, never touch the meat, but keep all the other dogs away.

That was a happy life, going to sleep with the wolves howling around or fighting the dogs in the back yard. The dog would chase them away, then they would chase him back. It was common for him to bark treed in the yard on small game during the night till we would get up and throw a tub over the animals till morning.

There was a concrete dam which overflowed from the Hyde's pond (the Hydes were neighbors who had several unusual features on their place including a greenhouse, which was the first glass building in our area, and which my father helped to build). In the spring rains, fine cat fish would wash over the dam and lodge in the large rocks in the road, Centennial Avenue. Old Tip found out we wanted those fish; he would listen to them flapping their tails, and bark treed, so we could reach back in the rocks and pull them out. Tip was also the best possum, skunk, and pole cat dog I ever knew. Game was plentiful, and in the hunting season he would tree them faster than we could skin them. (We sold our furs to Tom Kelly Poultry and Cream, corner of 5th and Lincoln, and to Wiel Fur Buyers on 4th between Howard and Grant in those days.) He would hunt till next morning, then he would be so tired he couldn't get up. I would stand him up and rub him till he could walk. By night he was eager to do it all over again.

During the dry summers a lot of wells dried up, and people watered stock and carried water from our well. My friend, Lawrence, had an Aunt Cary, who did washing at our well under an old cherry tree. A time or two I climbed up in the tree and dropped wild cherries in her wash water! She caught me one day when I climbed down and we really had a fight.

Robert, too, lived close by and went to school with us. He had a retired race horse he used to drive to the buggy. If that horse could catch any of us kids in the pasture he would get a mouth full of hair and lift us off the ground and then let us down, and when we would run he would do it again!

The phone rang one morning about breakfast time and father answered. Marvin Porter told him a mountain lion had tried to catch old Mack, the race horse; Mack broke out and ran through the yard and across the corner of Robert Porter's porch. (Remember the old crank phones? Porter's number was 908 and ours was 599 on the old line. I was phoning one day and it was storming; the lightning ran in on the line and sent me flying across the room.) About that mountain lion phone call — Mr. Porter said their little dog, Carlo, was having a fit in all the excitement! Mother tried to make Dad stay home, as he had to go that way to work. But Father only laughed and said it would take more than a mountain lion to keep him home from work. He had only his bicycle and had to walk up a little hill; the lion was sitting there watching him, but did nothing!! The next day we kids went and looked; we could see his tracks. We were hunting on Center Creek one night when a mountain lion screamed right over our heads. We had a lantern, and old Tip came and walked by our sides. As soon as we left the timber, the lion quit following us.

We got a break every summer tenting out for a few days at the old auditorium in Chautauqua Park, northwest of Carthage. The Church of God Reformation held a camp meeting with wonderful preaching, but what we kids enjoyed most was the camping out and eating differently for a few

Marshal Hooker's love for the outdoors is still strong. Here he and his wife, Katy, are seen at the Tennessee Longhunter's Rifle Frolic in April, 1981.

days. The auditorium was a huge building with no sides, bought from the railroad company. Pigeons nested up high on large timbers and we thought it was fun to see the people below wiping their heads and looking up, then moving over a little. There was a large watering tank with ice water and tin cups tied all the way around with strings, and a big, old cook shack.

There was a converted infidel, Willis M. Broun, a very bad man, who came to town to preach in the old church at Grand and Chestnut. He preached a lot in the winter and Mother wanted to go. Dad was tired from his day's work; the other kids didn't want to go, so I hitched up old Charley, and Mother and I went. Some nights were cold, windy and dark; other times it was bitter cold and the buggy wheels would whine and sing in the snow; the full moon made the night beautiful like a fairyland.

One of the boys who went to school during my days was named Hill P. He liked to be bragged on, so we would brag on him, telling how he liked to eat grasshoppers. Then we would catch the hoppers and the kids would crowd around and watch him eat them. He said they were good and would smack his lips. I caught some for him, but it made me sick to see him eat them. There were huge American Elms in the school yard and often the football would lodge in the high limbs. All we had to do was tell everyone that Hill wasn't afraid to go up and get the ball, and he would go right up and get it for us. The teachers would come out and plead with him to come down and he would laugh at them and go right on, till some of the limbs bent so much I knew he would kill himself; he always made it!

Sometimes on Sunday we would choose sides and have a battle with corncobs soaked in the water tank. A good solid hit could lay you out! And we had an old hack running gears that we put a seat on, with a rope line on the front axle. One person would sit on it and the others would push him down the hill real fast. There was a huge pile of cotton or field rocks at the bottom; when this light hack hit those rocks, it would go flying up into the air — much worse than any bucking bronco. Some warm nights we would go over into the large pasture and catch a bunch of milk cows; someone would get on and go flying through the brush until the cow bucked or knocked him off, then someone else would try. The next morning the neighbors would complain about their cows being wild and "off their milk." They thought maybe the dogs had run them all night, or the wolves. Of course, WE knew nothing about it!

We worked awfully hard at times, but it was a good childhood, with the best parents ever and a good, clean, country life — plenty of hunting and horseback riding. I grew older, and stopped hanging my sisters' dolls, stopped throwing my knife at their feet and sticking it in the floor or ground to hear them scream. Bertha didn't get too excited, but Mable would always scream, dance, and plead. I know now that she did that to please me, and wasn't scared at all. Although I was happy there and then, I suppose I couldn't know how good it was. Now there are many improvements in living conditions and travel, for me at least, but it was a better time then than now. I'm remembering now the many hunts at night for years with my faithful old dog. No more! I could drink out of springs, there was no adulterated food, anyone who wanted to could carry guns, and there were all kinds of good clean entertainment. We never heard of "pot" or "grass." The kids didn't want that kind of life. Most boys had a flock of bantams, or pigeons, and hunting dogs, and would trade and visit in a good, clean way.

Even then, as I grew older, I could see people changing. Now I look back at the golden childhood days, at the old kerosene lamp shining through the window. Warm summer nights just sitting in the yard, happy just to be with each other, and pleasantly tired from our day's work, or in the wintertime the lamplight through the window on the snow as we worked in the barn feeding and haying the stock, going in and eating a good homecooked meal. Mother patching our clothes and Dad playing his French harp — old songs like "Come to Me, Sweet Marie," "Little Mohee," "Nellie Gray," "Old Folks at Home," "Silver Threads among the Gold," "Babes in the Woods," "Old Black Joe." Mother sometimes playing on the old pump organ, or reading a book to me. Sometimes Uncle Renzy would walk out from town and bring his cylinder record phonograph and play it; people would come from all around to listen. That was living, simple, clean, with love for each other. Even the hard work, now that I look back on it, was enjoyed, but I didn't realize it then.

There was much hard work, really hard, like driving old Dolly, or any one of the other horses, south to Center Creek (six miles) to get a load of poles for the cook stove and heating stoves. We had two sets of lines so we could run behind our wagon on the way home, facing the north wind, trying not to freeze. While resting for dinner in the woods, we would catch a few flying squirrels that tamed readily and made good pets. We carried our water up the hill in gallon buckets, or pulled eight of them in a little wagon, with lids on them to keep the water from splashing out. Some warm evenings when Mother was tired she would sit on the west side of the house in her little rocker which I still have, and read. The air was pregnant with the smell of her nasturtiums and other flowers. Dear God, what I would give to see them again and live just one day like we did then!!

Chapter III

ABOUT Carthage — the Osage Indians occupied this area when it was first discovered by the white man. An area bounded by a line two miles east of Carthage was ceded to the U.S. in 1818, the line running north and south. In 1825, five years after Missouri became a state, more land around Carthage was given up by the Indians.

French explorers were in this region in 1719, and Spanish explorers were here before that. Thus southwest Missouri has been under 6 flags: French, Spanish, French Republic, U.S., and for a time the Missouri flag in 1861, then U.S. again.

It is thought that the first white man to come into this area was Edmond Jennings from Jackson County, Tennessee. He came and stayed fifteen years, living with the Osage Indians; he walked and came alone. Arthur Onstatt came in 1833. Then others followed. The nearest mail was Little Piney, 150 miles east. Everyone had to walk, ride horses, or use wagons with horses or ox teams. Most tried to settle around springs and most houses were of logs. The pioneers made out the best they could on what they could raise or make. Supplies had to be brought from St. Louis — a trip of five to eight weeks!

Carthage was a planned city — on March 8, 1841, James Nickoles was the first to survey for the city and was paid $10.00. Henry Piercy built the first home, north of Carthage on Spring River in 1833. The first courthouse was built in 1841 of logs and is now owned by the Sheldon family northwest of Carthage on its original site. The second courthouse was erected in 1842 by Levi and Jenkins, costing $398.50, a two story frame house with a fireplace and on the north side of the square. Lots around the square sold for $10.50 to $44.00 at that time, with two months' credit. In 1854, a brick courthouse was built in the center of the square, costing $4,000. This one was destroyed in the Civil War, in 1863.

Shirley's Tavern was on the north side of the square. John Shirley, the owner, was the father of Myra Bell Shirley, later known as Belle Starr, the woman bandit. The Carthage House (the Shirley Hotel) was moved from the north side of the square to Howard Street, east of the square, then to the present location by two of my uncles, with horses pulling it all the way. The present courthouse was built in 1894. My father cut a lot of the stone and helped build it. He also helped build the High School on Grand, the Carthage Public Library, and many of the Carthage stone sidewalks still used today.

There were thirteen engagements at Carthage during the Civil War; the famous Battle of Carthage was on July 5, 1861. And there were many outstanding local individuals during the war — one such was known as the "Buckskin Scout." His last name was Hood. There were many more, but in a book such as this, it is impossible to mention them all.

Some early businesses were: the Morrow Milling Company, 1848; Carthage Foundry, 1861; Carthage Press, 1872; Legget & Platt, 1823; Carthage Marble Corporation, 1850 (quarries of white limestone and grey marble — world famous); Frisco Railroad, 1872; Missouri Pacific Railroad, 1880.

It is said that after the Confederate guerillas destroyed Carthage on September 22, 1864, there were only three buildings left standing. People returning afterwards saw wild deer drinking from the horse watering troughs on the square. All new homes had to be built — few former residents returned. Some who did were Norris C. Hood, Mrs. McCoy, Thomas G. Glass, Dr. A. H. Caffey, J. W. Young, M. M. James, Mrs. Elwood B. Jones, Dr. John A. Carter, Dr. Robert Brooks. Most of the following, prominent in Carthage history, were newcomers at this time: W. H. Phelps, A. M. Drake, Thomas Gray, William Wright, Peter Hill (who was mayor in 1890). Later buildings erected were the Harrington Hotel, Carthage Woolen Mills on North Main, Carthage Ice and Cold Storage, Platt Plow Works, Carthage Foundry, Steward's Studio, Stanley Lumber.

The first school began in 1867, taught by Andrew J. Shepard and his sister, Mrs. George Orner. Then came the old Central School, Benton, Washington, Irving, Franklin, Columbian, and Carthage Collegiate Institute. Later came the Mark Twain, Eugene Field, and the old red brick Central schools. There was the Bank of Carthage, 1868; the First National Bank, 1872; Farmers and Drovers Bank, 1875; Jasper County Bank, 1875, and Central National Bank, 1890. The first railroad, Memphis, Carthage & Northwestern, 1872, was later sold to the Frisco line in 1879. The Missouri Pacific Railroad, 1880, connected Carthage to Kansas City in 1889. A. H. Rogers built a mule street car line, then organized the Southwest Missouri Electric Railroad, going from Joplin to Webb City to Carterville. In 1896 it was purchased by the Jasper County Electric Railways, linking Carthage, Carterville, Joplin, Pittsburg (Kansas), Pitcher (Oklahoma). This line I have ridden many times.

The first newspaper was the *Carthage Pioneer*, published by James Kelly in 1857 and sold to C. C. Dawson who changed it to *Southwest Star*. In 1866 Thomas M. Garland founded the *Carthage Weekly Banner*, which later became the *Carthage Evening Press*. Also there was *Carthage Democrat* by C. Conrad and A. W. St. John (who published the *Press*); these men then sold to W. J. Sewell and E. L. Dale.

Elmer Camel, one of the best horsemen that ever lived, helped me remember some of the old places. Robert W. Opp Livery Stable — horses, buggies, and teams for hire, also bought or sold. Pearl Roller Mills, Missouri

Woolen Mills, Carthage Woolen Mills, Caston Brothers Photograph Gallery, Eagle Mills, Carthage Opera House, Corothers & Deals & Black Drugs — watches and books. The old water well on the northeast corner of the square where anyone could get water, the chains for tying your horse on the square, the green iron watering troughs, the old brick mill where we bought clay for 10¢ a load, old water works on branch of Spring River, Blacksmith Shop at 5th and Main, Jack Aiken & Miller Livery at 2nd and Howard, Bibee Livery between 2nd and Central, Blacksmith Earl Black & Jim Porter on Central, Mabee & Pike Blacksmith on 4th Street, Hall Livery Barn on 4th and Garrison, Hunter Feed Barn, Miller Feed Barn, George Kuntz Livery Yard, McFadden Feed Yard and Rental between 5th and 6th, taken over by Brochus & Tangner, Perkins Feed Yard on Central. The old scales between Elm and Meridian, and the old bell mill on Meridian. The old Star Mill (where I bought feed many times as a boy); much of this mill is now part of the old mill at "School of the Ozarks." Lampher Brothers Carriage Shop on Grant, Turner's Carriage & Harness on the south side of the square with the big gray horse out front, with harness or saddle on. (A set of harness was $17 or $18 then.) Perry & Wilson Feed Barn on Central, Aetna Hotel for the drummers, Carthage Hotel at Mound and Main, Metcalf Blacksmith Shop, where I had a lot of shoes put on my horses in those days. Al Rose Feed Yard, Wiel Fur Buying on 4th Street, Tom Kelly Fur Buyer at 5th and Lincoln, and I sold a lot of furs to both places. And there was Patterson Feed on 2nd and Grand, Tucker's Feed Store at Howard and 3rd, which is now Cantrel's.

I never rode on the old mule car, but it was 5¢ a ride — south on Main to Macon and down Grand to the Square. My uncle Robert Hooker drove the water wagon to sprinkle in front of the houses in the dusty summer time, 5¢ to 10¢ a yard; he could fill the wagon with water for 25¢ and 50¢.

A Mr. Tangner had a farm southeast of Carthage where some famous race horses were bred and trained — among them was "Cold Deck." This farm was the old Buller place. Our little buckskin mare, shipped in from the west, was bred at Tangner's place every year to a fine stallion named "Captain Jupiter," a beautiful bay; but we got buckskin colts every time. At the livery stable on 4th and Lincoln, an Indian named Mongo would ride any bronco for a buyer for $2 till the critter stopped bucking — that was rough broke. The broncos sold for $5 to $20 apiece.

Carthage had its share of saloons, but I never knew too much about them. I remember drunks on the streets, but no women. One saloon was on Main, just off the square, one on South Main between the square and 5th east side, and one on 4th where Sober Tailors were in so long, on the south side of the street. I had a sign out of that place which read, "Don't swear in here. It sounds like hell!"

At the Ragen Place on Central there was a spring where the water was supposed to be good for your health; they sold that water for 10¢ to 25¢ a gallon.

The first Chief of Police I remember was Jasper Hawkins, a pretty good old man; and he arrested me for riding my bicycle on the sidewalk one day when I rode to town. Then I remember Jesse Means, who came to church to keep things quiet. There were a few young punks who liked to disturb the services and old Jesse would sure make them scatter.

Well, one could go on and on, but that is plenty about early Carthage.

Chapter IV

THE next best thing to being an old timer is having the opportunity to know and listen to those who have lived with the old timers. The stories I heard from the old folks impressed me very much. There were many stories — about good and bad people, animals, and weather. Some have made a real difference in my outlook on life; some are merely bits of historical interest.

When my mother lived on the Oklahoma prairie, they kept coyote pups. One day they fixed dinner and left it on the table while they went to church. It was hot and they left the door open a little; the pups got in and got hold of the tablecloth and dragged it all off on the floor. When I was young I just had to have some coyote pups to raise, too, and my mother allowed it.

There was always something rather wild and exciting going on! Two of my relatives by marriage would go into a bar and start a fight, running everybody out. Then there was the man who would shoot a glass of whiskey off his friend's head with his pistol. I liked to see Mr. Rainwater, with his long hair like Buffalo Bill, in his bar in the hotel on the northeast corner of the square. A man came in there one day and said, "I want the best drink in the house!" Mr. Rainwater gave him a glass of water. On a hot summer day, a Mr. Black went into the saloon and asked for a beer. The bartender refused to wait on him, so Mr. Black grabbed that bartender, lifted him over the bar, hit him once with his fist, and killed the poor man. In Stotts City, where Emmet Poindexter was a lawman, a fellow cut another man's stomach open with his knife. The injured man picked his intestines up off the street and carried them to a doctor; the doctor washed them clean, sewed him up, and he lived!

There was a saying, "Everything was wild, including man." In Joplin, a bad man, Joseph Thorton, was so bad that he was in a class all by himself. And for a long time, without being bothered, he was a bootlegger in Kansas, a gambler in Missouri, and a drunkard who reveled in red liquor. He would ask someone to shoot the ashes from his cigar while he blew smoke rings. He would set his bottle of beer or whiskey on a fence post and shoot the neck off, and then drink the liquor. Deputy Sheriff Julius Miller, Big George McMarty, and a sixty-year-old Irishman, Dad Sheehan, went into the famous "144 Saloon" to arrest Thorton. Well, Thorton shot and killed poor old Sheehan and almost killed Deputy Miller. Big bad Thorton was finally subdued and locked up. When the word got around, the people gathered and broke into his cell. The leader said, "Come on, Joe. Sorry to disturb you, but we have to do this."

"Don't mention it," said Joe. Under a tree limb they asked him, "Do you want to make your peace with God? This is your last chance." He said, "I have forgotten all my prayers." So up he went!

Then there was the Carthage sheriff, Buck Rock, who got shot and killed, and the rich lawyer who got one eye shot out, doing what he should not have been doing. These "going's on" were all around, and happened every day. Two black men were burned, tied to a tree (a big locust on ground I later owned) for molesting a white woman.

People were always getting into it over something, and mostly over something foolish and unimportant. Like when my Uncle Tate lived in the house that used to be "The Carthage House," at the present location of the Shirley Hotel. My cousin and I were fooling around there one day, and got into a little difficulty and I broke his arm! Why do people have to be so foolish?

We used to hurry out of church as soon as we could after the sermon, and put the tugs on the outer edge of the singletree. The older people would come out and start home. The shaves would drop down, the horse would tear around, and they would have a time! Or, we would put rocks about three feet apart in the muddy ruts; the buggy wheels or Model T Ford wheels would hit them and nearly throw the passengers out on the ground.

I was getting older and went to work at the Menerva Candy Kitchen, on the west side of the square, which was run by two Greeks, Andrew and Theodore Klenzoes. We made enormous batches of candy, and ice cream by the huge freezers full. There were huge marble top tables where we rolled and shaped candies. Sometimes I would catch one of the many cats in the building and glue half of a walnut on each foot with glucose, then pitch him on to the hard stone tables. The slipping, falling, and squalling was really something to see and hear!

While I was working at the candy kitchen, one morning real early while we were about to clean up after working all night, a young man came in. We knew him; he ate a few pieces of candy, then left. Later he was convicted of killing a man that night and throwing the body into the river at Tucker's Ford, northwest of Carthage. But while they were hunting for the suspect, before they caught this young fellow, the police were bringing in any stranger to question. Two policemen at that time, Mike Horgan and a Mr. Morgan, did not like each other at all. One of them brought in a man he suspected and the other one made fun of him. It ended up with both men pulling their pistols; the people were so thick they couldn't get a bead on each other. But the people scattered, and some of the older heads got hold of those two policemen and kept them from shooting.

I also worked with my Uncle Renzy getting the wiring fixed at the old Knell Fair Ground, so there would be electric lights. This was northwest of the city. And I also helped take up tickets when we hauled people out there in flat bed trucks. There was horse racing and all that goes on at a fair — balloon ascension, and an old man who would butt heads with a billy goat. He put his head down once and a sharp "horse weed" that had been cut off, stuck in his nose and killed him. Then there was the man who put horse shoes on his shoes and pulled a cart around from place to place, eating grass and nickering like a horse.

Mr. Lamb, a relative of my grandmother, was a lawman in Sarcoxie. He went into a pool hall on the west side of the square to arrest a mean fellow. This man had no intention of being arrested. After a few hard words, they both went for their guns, and Mr. Lamb had to kill the man.

There was a man in jail in Carthage for murder, and the time was set for his hanging. No one believed he was guilty, except a few — and the jury. He was allowed to walk out of the jail so he could escape. Instead, he spent the night fishing on Spring River. He came in next morning and was hung. He said that he did not commit the crime, but was not going to run and hide the rest of his life.

Before my time the Daltons, James, and Youngers had a place to stay at different times in Carthage on the northeast corner of Chestnut and Valley. The Daltons came into the Bank of Carthage several times and it was thought that they had intentions of robbing it. The bank ordered several Winchester rifles and Colt revolvers, and these were kept handy by the men working in the bank. But the Daltons went instead to Coffeeville, Kansas, and tried to rob two banks at the same time; only Emmet Dalton survived, and he was all shot up.

Life was going along about as usual. My older brother, Merrill, was to be drafted in World War I, in the next draft. Then one night (towards morning) we heard bells and whistles in the clear night air, and we knew something important was going on. It was November 11, 1918. The folks got on the old grinder phone and learned that the war was over. We got up, harnessed the horse and went to town. I shall never forget that day — the square was full of people laughing, crying, and drinking. The hardware stores opened their doors, handed out guns to anyone and put boxes of cartridges on the counter for anyone to use free. This sounded like a battle! Someone would put a gun in my hands and tell me to shoot, and believe you me, I would shoot. When night came all the ammunition was gone and the gutter was full of empty shells. It was a great day of rejoicing! And I never did hear of anyone even being injured in all the wild shooting. We didn't have crazy anti-gunners around then; there was still some freedom left.

About this time my father decided to move to town. We had a Model T Ford and it was hard to start — we pushed it up and down the hill trying to start it so many times. I decided it was easier to walk. I don't blame him, for after working all day and riding his bicycle home, it was a hard way to go. But I didn't want to leave the old home place. I had no choice, so we got rid of the livestock, and in the dead of winter moved to 602 Lincoln Street in Carthage, Missouri. On my last trip in, I brought my mother and little brother Lee to town in a raging blizzard. It was all I could do to make "Old Charlie" face the storm. I was upset leaving my old home, as I loved it very much. I never did, and still don't, like city life.

Marshal Hooker before going on a hunt in the 1960's.

During the rest of the winter I went to school and walked out in the country to hunt. But life wasn't the same. My hunting dog, "Old Tip," and I didn't know what to do with ourselves most of the time. As time went on I decided town wasn't for me, but I stayed until spring — I was twelve years old then.

On June thirteen I landed in Oklahoma; it was my birthday and I was thirteen now. I worked through harvest, then plowed long fields of cotton, wheat, or prairie ground with a gang plow or sulky. This was so different from home, no rocks or stumps and no more walking. These were riding plows, a new experience for me.

The prairie was absolutely a solid mass of buffalo wallows. I rode over to the place where Mother and her family took their claim, and I was able to pick out the places where several of the incidents she had mentioned took place when she was a girl. Then I went to herding cattle. Now this was more like what I had in mind all along. I had a white mare to ride who knew more about herding cattle than I did — a real honest-to-goodness trained cow-pony. Then there were "Bird" and "Ribbon," two dark red bays who were young and fast; and a tall grey gelding, "Old Dan," quite a stumbler but a willing worker. We never worked but a half day on Sunday; then I could hunt on the prairie. There were plenty of jackrabbits, lots of coyotes, and still a few wolves.

I decided to go back home and take one more year of school. I sure missed the good free life. I took my faithful old Tip and went hunting this winter in the snow. I walked in deep snow to Dryfork, north of Carthage, with rabbits tied around my waist. I froze my feet; they were black, and I went upstairs (this was in the home of the Harron's) on my knees to bed. In the night my feet hurt me something awful. I remember that for supper that night we had dried salt herring fish, and the other things that go with a country meal. Next morning I was still full of the old hunting spirit; after my feet got cold they quit hurting. So this day I walked on north to a little town called Kanoma; that now put me twenty miles from home. My feet were clear frozen, and I was starved, and the snow was deep. I went to the home of Marion Bruffet (a man who went to our church) to get a meal. He took one look at my feet and, after we had eaten, put me and the rabbits in the old Model T Ford and took me home. I didn't complain; I was thankful for that ride home.

When school was out I went to work for Alvy Tremble on a farm up by Lockwood, Missouri. We milked the cows and harnessed the horses before breakfast, in the dark. After that we would eat breakfast and work until too dark to see. After dark we cared for our horses and milked the cows again. Then came supper, but I was almost too tired and sleepy to eat. And this was for $15.00 a month. One day I plowed up a nest of hornets and the team didn't stop until they reached home.

After that I hauled river gravel out of a creek bed, to put on the country roads. The water was cold and I had to stand in it about knee deep to shovel the gravel into the wagon. The water was running down my arms and I was wet all day long, and about to freeze. I was strong and did a good day's work, but it was about to get me down. This man whom I worked for was a surly character anyway and thought I should get an extra load every day. Well, I was already working myself down trying to do a good job. This was too much, so I told him what he could do with his outfit and walked back to town.

I got a job putting in a bridge over Dry Fork, north of Carthage. It was very cold working over the frozen water. We drove to work in a Model T Ford. Just this side of the river, at a farm house, a huge dog would run out and try to bite me. We were in a touring car, with an open top, and the doors were not too high from the ground. One day the dog got too wild and too close for comfort; he meant business and his people would not call him back. So the next day when he tried the same thing, I put my hand gun in his face and let him have it; we never saw him after that.

I decided to go back to Oklahoma, for I liked that country. There were still a lot of Indians, cowboys, and other things I liked there. I went back again three miles southwest of Oklahoma City and herded cattle on the B.

C. Ranch. Had a little incident there: a man I never knew, and who had no reason as far as I knew, jerked out his pistol and emptied it at me point blank. I just stood there and after the first shot I counted as he fired. After his last shot, he ran. I went to the ranch house, got my six shooter, and headed back to his place, a very stupid move. But the ranch boss saw me headed for his place, intercepted me, and said he would take care of it, and gave me something else to do. I don't know how he took care of it, but I cooled down.

My boss and his pal, a fellow called Chris, broke horses for the Army in World War I, in Washington or Oregon state, I believe it was. His horses were used in several bank holdups. He was put in jail in Guthrie, Oklahoma, three times for helping Kid Wilson and Henry Starr rob banks in Oklahoma. He was staying in a place where Buffalo Bill was putting on his Wild West Show. One day Buffalo Bill was taking a nap in his chair in the sun on the hotel porch. Bill's mouth was open; my boss, Belden, cut a little stick of wood and stuck it between Bill's teeth. Bill jumped up and couldn't close his mouth. He yanked the stick out and said he would kill the man who did it, but soon cooled off.

Here on this ranch we boys would ride out on the quicksand on the South Canadian River. We had to force the horses onto it as they knew better. The water would come through the sand as we ran our horses and we would try to keep ahead of it. One day, Wayne Hayes got stuck and was going down. We had to pull poor Wayne out; I thought for a while we were going to lose him. Another pastime was racing our horses and jumping ditches on the prairie where water had cut down deep. We didn't always make it, sometimes falling back into the ditch, horse and all.

A man came to our place to kill our boss, who had gone to Oklahoma City. He said he would wait for the boss. I managed to slip out, get a horse and ride to meet the boss. I feel sure I saved one of their lives, and maybe both. These things were exciting at the time.

Chapter V

I MOVED to Copan, Oklahoma. It was known as one of the last real tough towns and was still a place where you didn't act mean unless you meant it. I went to work here for a man who lived outside town and worked for the road district. This was the year the big storm hit Seminole, Oklahoma. It tore shingles off our big barn and blew tools and things from our yard, and we never saw them again. My work was taking a team and going out in the fields, gathering sand rock, and hauling them to bad places in the road, fixing the holes.

The man I worked for was called Al. He had been a bank robber and Post Office robber and I don't know what else. On one occasion a lawman walked over to his place to arrest him. Just when Al saw the lawman coming, a jack rabbit jumped up in front of the officer and ran; Al raised his Winchester and drilled the rabbit; the lawman had second thoughts and went back to town. An Indian came to town one day and told Al he had come to whip him, guns, knives, or fists. They talked it over and decided on fists. The Indian took his guns and knife off and they went to the middle of the road and went after each other. It was a real bloody affair. Both were pretty well done in, tired and bleeding. Finally the Indian decided he could not whip Al. He struggled to his horse, put on his knife, guns and belt, and rode off. What this fellow Al did would fill a book. He had worked on the X I T Ranch in Texas and had a scar on his face that he got down there. He had been into more things, but was a likeable person, afraid of nothing, and as strong as a bull. My older brother lived in Copan. One day his car slid off the road into a ditch and Al shoved it back upon the road. Another time my brother had a flat; we had high pressure tires then, with clincher rims which took tools to get them over the rim. Al put both his hands over the tire and squeezed it together, raised it up, and pulled it off. He had pulled a job and was in a Model T Ford starting to leave. A lawman ran out with a shot gun and told the man at the wheel to cut the motor off, which he did. Al got out of the car, went around and pushed the lawman out of the road, cranked the Ford, shoved the other man over and drove off. The officer was asked why he didn't shoot and he said, "I couldn't shoot such a brave man."

We were riding one day and saw a fellow plowing over in a field a way off.

Al said, "Watch this." We stopped and Al went over to the fence and acted like he was going to talk to the man, who had other ideas. He stopped plowing and ran into the brush of a creek nearby. Al just laughed and we rode on. He never explained and I figured it was none of my business. I know of three of his bank jobs. Also he helped, fed, and took care of Al Spencer, one of the desperate outlaws in Oklahoma. Al had him in his barn hiding in the hay before he was shot down without a chance (betrayed by his friends).

There was always shooting going on. One of the local gamblers got his arm shot off in a game. And I liked to see a Mr. Young ride into town on his white cow horse. He had his yellow slicker behind the saddle, and was of the old school. He would come into the Post Office and get his mail almost every day. I was told he would leave every so often, be gone for awhile and come back. Once in a while he came back in a Dodge coupe, the one with the green star on the radiator. He was always quiet and didn't say much. (And I remember my Post Office box was No. 131 — the little box that had the dial and combination to remember.)

The constable's name was T. A. Malin; Justice of the Peace, J. W. Bartlett. The man I worked for had two sons younger than I was. If we were in town any time, noon or evening when school was about to let out, we would wait until the kids were strung along the broad sidewalk, then spur our horses down the line and the kids would scream and scatter. The old boards would break as three horses would pound on them, and it was a lot of fun. The lawman would try to grab my reins to get his hands on me, but I always escaped. He never tried to get the other two boys. After we had had our fun, we would ride on out of town. Then he would watch us the next time we were in town. Boy, did he ever get mad! We always put our horses up in Metcalf Livery Barn, and I stayed part time in Mrs. Metcalf's rooming house.

My boss and a young fellow robber held up a Post Office in Colorado. A posse chased them for miles; finally only one man was trailing them, the sheriff. He was mounted on a wonderful white horse. Al and the other man, Ernest Baldwin, knew their horses could not go much farther. They hid behind a cut bank and when the sheriff came up to them they got the drop on him and disarmed him. Ernest Baldwin had been admiring the sheriff's horse for some time, so he took the white horse and left his jaded old nag for the sheriff to get home on.

One day we were at home not working, and the conversation turned to shooting. Al went into the house and brought out a rifle. He did some shooting, then I did the same thing. The last thing he did was to put up a little rock about the size of a walnut out in the yard; he took the rifle and blasted it to pieces shooting from the hip. We put up another one and I shattered it the same way. It surprised everyone, and that ended the shooting match.

He and I were out on a scouting trip one night and were returning home. I was riding a big horse that was wild and crazy. Somehow or other, he got too near a fence and got caught in the barbed wire. I could see myself torn to pieces, but did some tall maneuvering to get us both loose.

Ralph Hooker as a youth at Pahuska, Oklahoma with headdress and blanket of head chief of the Osage tribe.

Al had a beautiful mare down in the Cotton Creek bottoms that could jump any fence, and would not stay penned up. She had a beauty of a colt, a real ivory color; and I bought it from Al. They built a large corral and the boys chased the horses in. The mare jumped six feet over the top bar, landed on her head and broke her neck, so we let the colt go for a while. Sad to say, but I was home in Carthage for a while and Al sold my filly, stole a Starr automobile and went west.

I was acquainted with a Delaware Indian man; he thought a lot of me. He told me about Cherokee Bill, the bad outlaw in Oklahoma, coming to his mother's place and asking for a meal. He always sat with his back in the corner of the room while he ate, his Winchester rifle, leaning by his side. My Delaware friend would go to church, and he always prayed in the Delaware language.

One of the finest men I knew was Tom Kitterman; there were several brothers, but Tom was my favorite. I stayed in his home a lot. He lived up a lane and I have seen him pick up a Winchester rifle and hold it ready when

Tom Kitterman and his wife — "One of the famous brothers that I stayed with in Copan, Oklahoma. When visitors came, he took his Winchester rifle to the door until he saw who it was."

someone came to the door. He had a very sweet wife and children. He had poor health but did what he could. At one time he had a small eating place on Main Street called "Tom's Place" where I ate whenever I was in town. He had the best fruit pie, and I ate like a starved wolf.

I recently visited Copan, and it was so changed I hardly knew the place. I stayed with Steve Shedd, who works for the city and is a part time lawman. I also visited with Tom Kitterman's married daughter, who looks like, and is, as wonderful a person as her mother was. And I met the present marshal. Everyone was so good to me, but it was sort of a sad visit — so many faces absent.

I used to sit in the evenings and listen to the men discuss their outlaw activities, and came up with the idea that I would show them how I could do it, too. I put it up to a friend, a full-blooded Cherokee, to help me. Everything was planned. I was going to rob the Copan Bank. I was going to go in and get the money and my friend was going to hold the horses. I was going to make a run for the Cotton Creek bottom. I had a place picked to bury the loot and not even the Indian knew where it would be buried. I knew I couldn't get away; they would catch me, but if I would cry and act real sorry, and be a good prisoner, I would soon be out, and then have some money to buy a ranch or something. I know now it wasn't the money I wanted, but the excitement and to show those older men I could do it, too. When the time came my friend changed his mind, wanted no part of it, and wouldn't hold the horses so I put it off. I was going to plan it again by myself, and not let anybody know my plans. I learned real early if you want to do something, do it alone, then no one can squeal on you; and then, no matter what, don't admit anything. Somehow or other, I got busy and just didn't get around to it, and more or less forgot about it. I almost was another one of those crazy fool kids who got his life fouled up over some stupid mistake right at the beginning. I never minded hard work and liked to work with my hands, so I must have just got my mind off the whole thing. I don't think I could have shot anyone in the bank; I am just not a killer. But I could have got a lot of hot lead myself. But anyway, I was "almost" a bank robber by age fifteen! I had by this time had quite a bit of experience for a youngster.

When I was at the B. C. Ranch, I hauled a load of freight from Oklahoma City to Watonga, Oklahoma. I loved to sleep with my outfit, sometimes in livery barns and sometimes in the open, so I could watch my things. My boss, Mr. Crowl, and I stayed one night out in the black jacks in the sand hills, close to Watonga, with some of his friends. Two other boys and I rode horses over to an Indian dance, a way out in the timber. The folks told us not to let the Indians see us, as they would be drinking and mean, and they didn't care too much for white boys. It was a dark night and we tied our horses back in the black jacks and crawled up pretty close to the dance. It was wild all right, drinking, singing and cursing, guns, knives, and fights. It was a really wild scene! It could have been a scene from the 1700's or early 1800's back in the east, before these Indians were so cruelly moved to Oklahoma. Maybe they remembered the unjust removal, the many deaths in freezing weather, being driven from their homes by greedy, unscrupulous whites who coveted their lands. And this was ordered by our President

Marshal Hooker at age 16 in Copan, Oklahoma. "Where I planned my first (and only) bank robbery but never carried it through."

Jackson; just one of the detestable acts of our U.S. government against helpless people. Indians who fought with Jackson in wars, and one saved him from certain death, pleaded with him not to send them away; but he had them put in stockades like animals, and driven west, making them come in wintertime. How cruel can the men in power be? No wonder the red man hates the whites. I think if I had been an Indian, I would have been the bloodiest fighter of them all, trying to save my homeland. After the awful tragedy, Jackson was known to the Indians as "The Chicken Snake."

But, back to the dance. The fires got bigger and the light got brighter and we kept backing up to be in the dark. The drums were beating and the dancing and singing in Indian tongue were a real experience. I wished I could join them, but knew better. After a long time we went back to our horses and started back to the wagons. The sand was deep and the horses made no sound except the squeaking of the saddles. We were loping along and ran head on into a group of Indians coming to the dance late. The horses collided and some flew off into the sand. I managed to stay in the saddle but I knocked a big Indian off his horse. He jumped up and before I could get going again, he lunged at me. He was already drunk and was so mad he was almost insane. He tried to drag me off my horse and it suddenly dawned on me that he was trying to kill me! I spurred my horse and kept beating the fellow in the face. It was all I could do to hold on, but in desperation I held onto the saddle horn with one hand, and kept clobbering him in the face and head with the other hand. I drug him in the sand and he refused to let go. Maybe the horse, which was real excited, stepped on his foot or something, but at long last I tore him loose and the other boys were ahead of me, waiting to see if I made it. They never offered to help; I guess they had their hands full for a while. I always wondered what that fellow was calling me, but I know it wasn't anything nice. Since it was in the Indian tongue, I didn't understand what he said — but pretty well knew what he meant!

The next morning before we left this place, the locals said they had a mule I couldn't ride. I thought I could, so we saddled him and I found one big spur and climbed on. As soon as I got on they set the pack of dogs, which were lying around the yard, on the beast. He bucked and kicked, and took off through the black jacks. Between the dogs, mule, and the brush, it was about all I could do, but I managed to stay on and circle back to the house. I was sure in a bad way, but they were surprised that I rode so well. They didn't know I had spent so many days on horses at the old home place.

I went back to see my folks in Carthage. Copan still holds a lot of pleasant memories, but I didn't move back there. I went to work in a shoe factory on River Street. This was inside work, which I didn't like at all, but I liked to work with leather. I was on the line where the leather passed from one person to another. Before they quit working there, I handled more pairs of shoes than any person in the history of the factory. I was working here when I was married in 1924.

Chapter VI

THERE is nothing like that first real love; when it happens and you get the girl of your dreams, life sure opens up a whole new happy way of living. I just knew I had the best and sweetest wife a man ever had.

I helped move the shoe factory machines from Carthage to Aurora, Missouri, and helped set the machines up. I worked for a while but didn't make enough money to rent an apartment. Several of us men stayed in a little hotel in the east part of town. We nearly froze at night as they refused to heat the rooms, and rent went sky high in the town when the people thought so many workers were coming to town. So, much as I hated it, I quit the factory.

I worked part time for a man putting in concrete sidewalks in Carthage. He was a very strong man. It was said that he killed a man in Kansas with his bare hands. He would let any man take a pair of pliers and pinch his nose if he could. He would have hold of your wrist and would squeeze it till your hand would be numb and lifeless. He was real good to work for, but in cold weather so much time was lost because the cement would freeze. Times were getting a little hard and there wasn't much work, so one day I went by his house to see if it was too cold to work and he said it was. We were in his barn and he had just finished milking his cow. He told me she was getting too old and not giving much milk so he guessed he would butcher her. I said, "Do you mean it?" and he said he did, so I pulled out my old Colt sixshooter and shot her in the head. He was so surprised that he stood there stunned for a while, then he came to. He said, "I never intended to do it now."

"Well," I said, "you'll have to do it now." He asked, "How will I get her out of the barn? I can't butcher her in here." I thought that was his problem and also remembered how strong he was; he was getting madder by the minute so I thought it was time to be moving on. He told me to come back and help him but I told him to get his son out of bed – he could help. I didn't fancy working with him, and him with a butcher knife in his hand. He might work on me instead of his cow. I went out in the country to shoot some rabbits with my sixshooter. He pulled the cow out with his string haltered horse and took care of the meat. I worked for him quite a while but he never liked me much after that. Did not see him then for a long time. I heard he was sick and didn't know if he would want to see me or not, but I went to his house. At first he had mixed emotions, then he began to laugh real big. He brought up the shooting of the cow; said it was the funniest thing he had ever seen. I was glad I visited him before he died.

I had different jobs around Carthage and times got harder and the Depression came on. We had one fine son and daughter. I think I was the happiest man in Carthage, but it was hard to find work when the Depression really hit. It was really bad; there simply was no work. We would drive the Model T Ford to the woods and work all day real hard — cut the trees down, saw, split and rick the wood for 75¢ a rick. And those were solid ricks, not like now, laid so you can see half empty spaces and call it a rick!

East of Carthage on the old Phelps place was a pasture with huge hedge trees. In the fall flocks of black birds would roost in the trees. I would get an iron chain, then throw a hedge ball in the tree and yell real loud. The birds would fly into the air (hundreds of them) then settle down low to find a limb to roost on. While they were all around me I would whirl the chain around my head and it would knock many of them to the ground. I would get a sack of them; we ate black birds till I would get sick when I would see one flying over. We ate opossom, rabbit, quail, or anything we could get. I got an old Harper's Ferry Civil War musket from Henry Ames, who lived on the east side of Budlong Street, and powder and musket hat caps from Carter's Hardware, and used them to bring in meat for us. A person did anything he could to get something on the table, and it led to some queer situations — too monotonous to explain.

I was hunting on Buck Branch and a fellow, from a distance of about a foot, snapped a 12 gauge shotgun in my stomach. It happened so quickly I didn't have time to move. I knew I was going to die and braced myself for the shock. The gun never fired; it wasn't the gun's fault and the load was good. Most people will think I am ignorant, but I know the LORD kept it from happening. Just like another time up by Sarcoxie — we were hunting and one of the boys was tired and in a bad mood. I just happened to look back to say something to him and found a 410 shotgun aimed at my head. I threw my head back and the charge just missed my face!

I had had words with a fellow I knew real well. He had been in the pen several times and had killed one man that I knew of. He said he would get me, so I carried my sixshooter, the same one I had shot the cow with, also the one I used to shoot cans off the head of Leo Earl for practice. I was going to town and met him on Budlong, between Orchard and Fulton Streets. I saw a wicked grin on his face. I could not fight as I had been injured and was taped from my waist up to my neck. (Funny thing, this was right in front of the church where I always went, even as a child.) There seemed to be no way out of it and I wasn't going to back down. I knew he carried a gun, also he was a boxer while in prison, and a real knife fighter. I walked from the sidewalk to the middle of the street and waited; he went to the street and came at me with that wicked "I got you now" grin. I always kept my gun under my shirt in my belt and my shirt unbuttoned there, so I could get in and out quick. I picked a spot on the ground which was close enough for him to come and when he reached it I was going to let him have it. I reached in and had my hand on my gun, ready to stop him for good. When he got pretty close, he stopped and we just stood there looking at each other for what seemed a very long time. Finally he got the message and went back to the sidewalk and left. The very next day I went to his house and bought some chicken eggs. Neither of us ever mentioned our near shootout and were friends — to a point. Later he was shot and killed; his luck had run out.

There was a man, Lon Clopton, who was quite a fighter himself, who also fought game chickens. One day some fellows went to his place, southwest of the city, to talk chickens. His were called "The Stinging Lizards"; they were pretty good! I know because I had fought against them. This day he wasn't at home. Before the men left, they opened the door to his house and put in a large billy goat that he had tied in his yard. You can imagine what he came home to! Talk about a mad man! He tried to find out who did it but no one ever told. You know I wouldn't have done a thing like that!

Right next to his place was a colored man, Walt Harbon. He had a fine race horse and would put it to a sulky and drive around in the evenings, which was a lot of enjoyment to him. He raised hogs and would gather garbage from town in his wagon. He came in one day and the man next to him had done something in the alley he didn't like. They got into a quarrel and the little man went into the house and got his 12 gauge shotgun and killed Mr. Harbon. I was told Mr. Harbon's mother was a slave as a girl on the 101 Miller Ranch in Oklahoma.

About this time, a friend of mine and I got to talking and wondered if we had a fight, which one of us would win. We figured there was only one way to find out, so we tried it. It was one of the hardest fights I ever had; he (his name was Cliff Wagnor) was some heavier than I and we were about the same age. We knocked each other around pretty hard for awhile. Then we rested and tried some more. We did this until we both were staggering and sick, and pretty well disfigured. I was considering a suggestion that we call it a draw, but didn't want to seem as giving up, for fear he would think after that he could whip me. Well, I sure was glad he thought of the same thing, and agreed with him — trying to act reluctant, but I couldn't have stayed on my feet for another round. We had no hard feelings over the fight.

I had a friend, a Mr. McCann, who was a jailer in Carthage. A man and woman came into the jail to release a prisoner, and killed my friend when he resisted; they fled. The woman lost a heel from one of her shoes as she ran down the steps at the jail. The affair was broadcast and a man in Chelsea, Oklahoma, saw a man and woman go into a restaurant — the woman had a heel missing. They were captured there.

One day a fellow who had shot at me with a shot gun and missed, came to our house with a bag full of money that was stolen. He wanted me to keep it for him and two other boys. I didn't want any part of it, but I did keep it hidden for awhile till the other boys were caught in Kansas. But I never accepted any of it!

Speaking of Kansas, I had been there on one of my trips before I got married. I worked for a German who had driven cattle up the Chisholm Trail, liked it in Kansas and stayed. We rode horses and herded cattle all around the west part of Wichita and Friends University. They called him the

"Flying Dutchman." A real old time cowboy, his name was Vestring.

Two young boys in Wichita had held up a man named Metcalf and killed him. They used an old S. A. Colt. One of the boys close to us came and tried to sell me an S. A. Colt 45 for $5.00. I didn't buy it. (He later became a lawman in Oregon, a real good one, too.)

Then I went to work for Hoover Orchards. They had apple orchards and also raised pigs, nice clean pigs in heated rooms and kept clean better than some people's houses. It was a very cold winter; I was put to work digging post holes and building fence out in that zero weather. Nearly froze. They never heated the upstairs where we slept and the nights were horrible. They fed us real good, but the old man tried to get through real quick, then wanted us all to quit eating and go back to work. His wife and two girls felt sorry for me and would keep me at the table and see that I had all I wanted, which made the husband furious. I didn't even have a coat to wear, and only summer underwear. My, how I suffered! There was a man working for him, living in a house on the place, with a wife and some children. The boss cussed this man from morning till night, the most foul language I had ever heard. I don't know why he didn't cuss me the same way, but he never did. One day I was in the pig house and the old man was cussing this hired man out. It was the most vulgar language I had ever heard a man use on another. I felt so sorry for the man being abused. I said, "I'll take a pitch fork and drive it through his guts. No man deserves what you are taking from him." The hired man begged me not to, but of course that ended my work there. The boss tried to run me off without pay after I had frozen and worked like a fool for him. I got up early next morning, and stole some money out of the house, to live on, and made myself scarce. I saw in the *Wichita Eagle* where the police were looking for me, but I made it back to Missouri.

We moved to Wichita later, and I went to work lathing and shingling new homes. Winter came again, and up on those houses it was another cold job. Some days it was absolutely too cold to work, and we would hunt rabbits for the market. I can remember one day we shot one hundred of them. We cut the entrails out in the middle of the road before bringing them to town. A farmer came along with a team of horses and they smelled the fresh guts in the road and tried to run away. The farmer wanted to do something to us, but had his hands full with the horses. That day we hunted in a farm yard north of Wichita where two old sisters lived. Those rabbits were so thick, sitting and running everywhere. You didn't know which one to shoot!

We also fought game cocks on Cow Creek. My employer here ran whiskey. We would park out in the country and make like we had car trouble. When certain people stopped to help we made the switch. But I thought that was a scroungy way to make a living and wouldn't go along with it.

Then trouble hit. I came down sick and we returned to Carthage so I could recuperate. When we first went to Wichita all I could afford to rent was a one room car garage. Slept on a pair of springs and mattress laid on a concrete floor. Either there, or hunting, or on top of the houses, I had caught a terrible cold. So when I got back to Carthage, I was in bad shape. My real trouble was appendicitis and I had lung trouble from the cold. We waited so long I had gangrene in my intestines. A Dr. Chapman and his son, also a doctor, had a hospital above Wells Drugs, southeast corner of the square. I went there to see if they could save me; they said I had no chance to live. I hated to leave my home, afraid I would never see my family or folks again. The ether would not put me to sleep because of my bad lungs. I told them to go ahead; I was anxious to get it over with. I was still awake when they cut in and started putting my insides on my stomach, then I fainted. Merrill, my preacher brother, was there and my folks and family and my Uncle Scott. The nurse came out and told them bad news, that I had stopped breathing and there was no chance. The doctors put their tools up. My father went in and told them to finish. The doctors argued that there was no need to operate on a dead man, but Dad said to go on and finish. Pretty soon the nurse came out again, real pale, and announced that I was breathing again. My uncle said they cut out ten feet of my intestines that had rotted and threw them away, and sewed up a lot of holes. My brother, pastor at Decoma, Oklahoma, said, "I preach divine healing to my congregation, and if it won't work when we need it, I won't preach it again." I know friends and the church were praying also. Now both doctors are gone, and I am still here. It took a long time to heal up, but with tender care and prayers and a world of patience, I finally made it. My wife fed me the best she could and never complained. So I owe my life to God, and to the people who made it possible for me to have time to heal.

Chapter VII

WE moved back to Yale, Oklahoma. I remember one day very well — it was like old times. They had a celebration in Cushing, Oklahoma — seemed like everyone there had a sixshooter on his hip. There was no law against it; there was a lot of shooting and fun and no one got hurt. I was surprised too, as there was a lot of drinking, and still several pretty bad men there. We were at Pawnee Bill's place, too, at Pawnee, Oklahoma, and he had five hundred wild buffalo in his front yard. I took June, my small daughter, out a ways to see a buffalo calf. Here came the calf's mother — head down and tail curled up in the air. We started for the house and I knew we couldn't make it. I pulled June down and we lay real still; the cow couldn't see us for the tall, blue stem buffalo grass. She went back to the herd and we got up and to safety.

There were some real genuine cowboys there. I saw some of them ride broncs till the blood ran from their noses and ears. I can still see the Indian women leading a goat down by the creek, then coming back after awhile with fresh meat in the middle of the goatskin, each woman holding a leg. Pawnee Bill treated us very well, and I enjoyed watching the Indians.

I lived one time at Pawhuska, Oklahoma, among the Osage. There was a man, Mr. Lamb, who dressed like a frontiersman and had a museum there. I spent a lot of time with him. The main chief, "Chief Bacon Rind," died while I was there. I had my picture taken wearing his personal beaded vest (which a Pawnee woman made for him) and his head dress, etc. John Stink lived in Pawhuska, too. He was a character — had many, many dogs. He was supposed to have died and they buried him; but he kicked himself out and came walking back, no worse for the burial!

We were also at Alluwe, Oklahoma, for awhile, where we lived next door to an Indian named Mose Paris. He had a son who could sure ride a horse bareback. And there was a white boy, Triplet, who was very much like an Indian living with them. The Indian boy kept beating up the white boy at the dances. One day the white boy decided he had had enough. When the Indian came up to start trouble, he was slashed across the throat, barely missing the jugular vein, and he went a long time all bandaged up. We were eating dinner one day and the stillness was shattered by rapid gun fire. The little Triplet boy dashed out of the house, and ran for the island in the Verdigris River; he made it all right, and wasn't even wounded. Three brothers in Alluwe robbed the local bank so many times that the bankers finally gave up and closed the bank.

I was wounded in Oklahoma and had to go home again to recover. I lay four years in bed. The doctor said I would never set foot on the ground again. My wife went to work at a garment factory to support our two children and me. She worked very long hours for $1.50 a day, and in all those hard trying times I never heard her complain once. I was in real bad condition — never ate in eleven days. I didn't eat and couldn't hold water on my stomach. A minister came to our place, anointed me and prayed for my healing. Of course, I didn't know how many more people were praying for me all along, but I threw my medicine away and in two weeks from then, I walked more than a mile to town.

A Mr. Cantrell, a retired doctor and poultry farm and hatchery man, lived on River Street, southeast of my place; I went to work for him. When I came home from Oklahoma that time I thought I would never work again. Now here I was working! (It makes no difference to me how many people think there is no God and if there is, He doesn't heal anyone; all I know is that He did it for me so many times! Even once when I was a boy and injured my foot and lock jaw had started in, the doctor wanted to take off my leg to save my life. My folks left it up to me and I said I would rather die than not to be able to run and hunt in the forest. They had special prayer that night when I was very low. Come morning, I got up and was all right.) The poultry business was seasonal, but between Dr. Cantrell and his two sons, I worked most of the year. They had the "Snow White Egg Farm" — wonderful people to work for.

I went to Casa Grande, Arizona, as a night policeman in the 40's when the big inch pipeline was being put across the desert. On the way there I had to pull my gun on two quarrelsome Yaqui Indians while riding the bus. Charles Post was Chief of Police, Gordon Hardesty, assistant chief, big Jack Milligan and I, patrolmen. Several other policemen were around, and some deputies and the highway patrol. But we four were the city police department. The FBI said the town of Eloy, twelve miles from Casa Grande, was the toughest town in the U.S.A. at that time. Someone had just killed the Marshal with a shot gun, and we had the whole bunch of rough ones in Casa Grande about every night. There were twenty cotton camps, five Indian reservations, plus the local elements and the pipeline crew. The old timers said it was wilder than when the Earps and the old gunmen were there. It WAS wild; there were killings and all kinds of fights.

I checked the businesses all night, and helped the other boys. Al Sizemore, the man whose place I took, found Stapely's Hardware front door open one night. He pushed the door open and the little bulldog that went with him on his rounds went in ahead of him. A man behind the door swung an iron bar down and broke the dog's back. They were crazy people! On Saturday nights the sidewalks were so crowded it was hard to walk on them. An Indian tried to rape a white woman in a crowd in the middle of the day. The chief picked me up and we found him headed for the shade of the water tank, south of Main Street. There were a lot of Indians gathered there, waiting for evening, to come to town and get wine. A lot of white people would buy it for them. They had their ponies tied up to the shrubbery around the tank. I ran and caught the man, supposed to be a bad Indian, (his name was Chico Thomas, and he had a wooden leg) threw him in the car, and he fought me all the way to jail. Another crazy Indian was beating his wife with a battery cable, trying to kill her because she was pregnant. I took him a long ways to jail and he fought me so hard that when I finally got him there, I was sick. And I had my "come on" chain on him, but he didn't seem to feel any pain.

The chief told me not to go in the 50-50 Club by myself, as it was a bad place, but I went in and brought out a Mexican man. These places were wide open — gambling, prostitution, drinking, and you name it.

The policemen surrounded an adobe house to capture a Mexican, and he was firing back. One policeman, Homer Ward, slipped up behind the shack and stood beside the back door, carrying a 38-40 single action. When the man came out Ward hit him on the head, and the hammer was on a full load; the gun went off and blew part of the Mexican's neck away. The assistant chief and I took in a huge Indian, wanted by the FBI. He was all right until we got him in jail, then he decided not to go any farther, and it took both of us to handle him. One deputy was after a man who was hiding between some boxcars at night west of town. The tracks ran through the middle of Main Street east and west; when the deputy shot, he missed the man and the bullet went up Main Street to where a Mexican woman sat rocking her sick baby. The bullet came through the wall, and went into the bedpost by their heads.

There was a white male who raped a white girl out behind a large sign on the desert at the edge of town. Before he left he took his knife and slit her breast open and left her to die. She managed to make it to the highway, and was picked up and taken to the hospital. We hunted this man, and three of us made a promise to each other; if any of us caught him we would make him fight so we would have an alibi for killing him. But he made it to another town before being caught.

I liked to be alone and work alone. I loved to run those dark alleys — some had no lights at all. There were a lot of poor children who would search those garbage cans for good food as soon as the business places would close; they always put everything back real clean and nice. Then when it was night, wild house cats would come in and go down in the barrels. When a person would come down the alley the cats would scatter for some hiding place. I knew if there were no cats, there was someone close and I could be on the lookout. The cats got used to me as I would throw them something to eat, and they got to looking for me and wouldn't run from me. So — if no cats, I knew someone was there in the dark. One way I got information was to go behind the jail, after I had put someone in at night (there was shrubbery to hide me) and I could sit down under the only window and listen. Nearly all of them would like to talk to the other fellows in jail, and some would brag about things they did or where some friend was hiding. I would come up with things and no one knew where I got the information. I heard one fellow tell the other men, "Don't fool around with that so and so from Missouri. he is mean and will kill you!" The most we ever put in that jail in one night was thirty-six, which was too many!

One day at the jail, Jack Milligan went into a cell with his gun on, which we were never supposed to do. One prisoner had set his mattress on fire. It didn't look right to me, so I went in after Jack. He had unlocked the cell door, gone in, and was cussing out the man who lit the mattress on fire, while helping to put it out. Another prisoner was on his bunk, lying down with his head to the passage. As Jack went in, this put him to Jack's back. When I stepped in the cell door, this man's hand was just closing over Jack's gun butt. I drew and put my 45 Colt S.A. in the fellow's face. He looked up so surprised — his eyes got real big, then his hand slowly came down away from Jack's gun. I have no idea but that Jack would have been shot in the back. I never did say anything to Jack and he never knew how near he came to getting killed.

Two of the policemen — I won't mention their names — got into an argument and both reached for their guns. I was standing near and it was none of my business. But when they went for their guns, I knew they were mad, and I knew they would not hurt each other if they had thought, so I jumped in between them and wouldn't get out of the way. I talked to them until they both cooled down and changed their minds about fighting. I never thought of getting hurt myself!

We had to attend what we called "Sheriff's meeting." They were evenings spent studying law enforcement procedures. One oldtimer said we were crazy to handle our rough ones the way we did. He said the old time officers wouldn't do that. He said the way so many policemen got killed was trying to handle the suspect by hand. One grizzled old time sheriff told me how he did it, and how the old fellows did it in the early days. He said he would tell the suspect he was under arrest, then toss a pair of hand cuffs to him and say, "Put these on, you ____," and if the fellow wasn't going to do it, he pulled his gun and shot the guy. I agree that is the way you should do it, but nowadays, if a policeman even roughs up a suspect, although he is a murderer or the worst kind of criminal, the policeman is suspended until they investigate. The poor prisoner must not be roughed up!

For a long time now we have had a bunch of narrow-minded liberals trying to take guns away from citizens. They always dream up a lot of lies and misrepresentations about hand guns, mostly, too ignorant to mention. We know the police can't be everywhere to protect us, but they insist that law abiding people must give up their means of defense. We might hurt ourselves or have accidents; we are more apt to get killed if we have a gun, as we don't know how to defend ourselves. So taking away from the law abiding will stop all crime! Hogwash! Some are even trying to disarm police. If guns are so dangerous, why do criminals endanger their own lives by having them? Their argument is too stupid to argue about. What they really want is to have a people that can't fight back, like other countries who are in bondage. How long would the Communist butchers last in Russia, if everyone had guns? Why did England beg us for handguns when the Germans came to their homes? They also say the second amendment of our

Marshal Ralph L. Hooker — police officer.

Constitution does not guarantee our rights to own firearms. They know that is a lie, but it is believed by some simple people who can't reason for themselves. They take polls and say seventy-five percent of the people want this or that; all they do is talk to the people who share their views or slant the questions so that you will answer like they want you to. If you want to know the truth and why we have so much crime, you can lay it directly at the doors of our crooked lawyers and judges. Only this week in New York, a man was sentenced to one year for stealing over one hundred thousand dollars, by a Judge Roberts. Look at the way some poor boy gets ten or fifteen years maybe, for stealing a ring, or maybe smoking a little grass. I know what I am talking about. I arrested a state's Attorney General for drunken driving and he was already on bail for taking gambling bribes. Do you think I got to lock him up?

At another time, Vick Poindexter and I had a real battle with a sheriff and his deputy. They were making and selling whiskey from the jail basement. We shot their car up while they were shooting at us and there was a lot of screaming. I don't know if anyone was hurt or just scared. Their car was disposed of. I went to town the next morning and told the police what happened, and I wasn't going to give the law any troubles, I just wanted to tell them what happened. They told me to go home, keep quiet, and forget it!

I know a lawyer in my neighborhood who is about as low as a man can sink. And he is practicing, and people trust him like he was somebody, and I dare say he is a bigger crook than anyone he has sent up. While I was a policeman in Carthage, I caught him in things that would have got anyone else in the pen, or killed, and he is only one out of many that I have found out. No wonder we have so many hoodlums in our cities and government — the ones in power do what they want. Right is right and no matter who you are, wrong is wrong!

I mentioned Carthage again; I was offered a deputy sheriff's commission at Eleven Mile Corner, north of Casa Grande, Arizona, and some talked to me about running for Chief of Police in Casa Grande. But I was having trouble at home, so I returned to Carthage, and the pipeline had moved to Buckeye, Arizona. I went on the police force in Carthage for almost six years. This again was all night work except when I helped the other policemen out or worked their days off. I walked around that old square many a time, ran a lot of dark alleys and open business places, and froze a lot of cold nights. I was at a gun show the other day and a fellow came up and said, "I know you; you put me in jail in Carthage once." I had got him out of a car one cold night from a car lot. I kept at this kind of work for so many years, that I began to think I should do something else for a change.

Chapter VIII

WHILE I was on the police department in Carthage, I arrested a young fellow stealing from the safe in Gale Earp's place, where he worked. When people think of the Earps, they at once think of the OK Corral fight. I knew George Earp, who spent his last years in the Old Connor Hotel, pretty well, and visited with him just before he died at the Elmhurst Rest Home. George was a first cousin of Wyatt Earp and was with him in Dodge City, Kansas. He saw W. shoot his first man and told me a lot of the early day happenings. George was a kind man, quiet, and I know he was honest. The last time I saw him before he died at the rest home, he was crying and couldn't get his shirt on. I helped him dress. He was in Kansas when the town of Ulysses was started. He was the first mayor which also made him the first marshal. He told me of being in Dodge when the trail herds came in. One boy was with a herd and was going home when the cattle were sold and he was paid. Another bunch of cowboys were there from another herd and the two outfits had words. One man from the last bunch took his Bisley Colt and shot the boy in the head.

At another place a man got off the stage with a plug hat on, and some boys across the street wanted to have some fun. One said he could shoot the man's hat off; he tried it, and shot the man in the temple. The man didn't die right away, so they put him on a pool table and played cards all night waiting for him to die, while one of them rode to another town to get a coroner. The poor fellow lived all night, but never came to. It was classified as an accident.

George told me while he was marshal in Ulysses there was a bad gunman who was giving him lots of trouble. He was staying with a woman in an upstairs room in town. George and a friend went upstairs to arrest him and found him still in bed. The woman made a dive for the man's gun and belt hanging on the foot of the bed. They grabbed her and made him stay down. He told them if they would not put him in jail, he would leave town, so they gave him until noon. At noon, the man and woman came dashing out of the livery stable in a buggy. The woman whipped the horses and was driving. They dashed down Main Street and out of town, the man shooting his big guns as they left.

Now when you go in a room after somebody, they have all the advantage.

Everyone sees you coming, but you have to locate them. I went into a large bar in El Paso, Texas, after a man. My gun was in my belt under my coat, but I had no more than come in the door than it was quiet as a church. I knew there were a lot of people there that needed arresting, and no one knew who I was looking for. Believe you me, there were a lot of mean characters there. I had never been there before; how they knew I was a lawman I don't know. For example, I was standing on a street corner in a little Kansas town one time, and I noticed a bunch of men across the street arguing. Finally one of them came across and said, "We were arguing about you; some say you are a minister and some say a lawman — you have to be one." Well, back to the bar in El Paso; I made my rounds — the whole circle, through tables and all, and no one moved or spoke. But if looks could kill, I could have died right there. The man I wanted was not there so I walked out. As I left, I heard the noise start up again. I found my man in Arizona.

There was a gunman in Arizona, by the name of Billy Stiles. They had him in Casa Grande jail once; no one would even bring his meals to him unless he would sit on the floor of his cell while the cell doors were open. He was later a night lawman in Casa Grande; when I was there I had the night job he had. Would you believe, some of the oldtimers that remembered him said I did a better job than Stiles did?

I can think of so many things that happened in the "not so long ago" and I don't want to be monotonous, but might mention a few. I hope they are taken like I mean for them to be. I am aware that I could exaggerate a little and make some fabulous statements, but I am trying to be conservative and also be honest. I realize I will have to give account for the truth in my writing or face it someday as a liar. I give credit for my good physical condition to my not drinking, very short time of smoking, and no very bad habits. In my fifties I had a friend, a Mr. Hartman, from New York City. He had a heart attack and could not work much. I used to take him hunting in Missouri in the brush pastures, and I would run rabbits around so he could shoot them with his 410. I have run a lot of rabbits down and caught them with my hands.

In the past I have put some loud, blustering rowdies in jail, and it was funny how quick some of them became mild; some of them even cried when the jail door clanked shut. I was coming home from the harvest field in Kansas one time, riding the freights to save money. The train stopped for water and I got off to stretch my legs. I saw two fellows trying to rob a boy in another car. This made me so mad I jumped them and ran them off, after a fight. The boy's name was James Sutton, from Lucern, Indiana. His buddy with him in the harvest field had stolen his money and gone home on the train, and James was broke and trying to get home. He gave me a nice belt buckle and a pair of spurs he got in Big Lake, Texas; I have tried to locate him to give those things back, but to no avail.

I was on the Mullendor Ranch in Hula, Oklahoma, and a horse ran away with a daughter of one of the ranch hands, and I overtook her. I was riding a very fast buckskin gelding. Big white rocks were everywhere. I let the horse have his head and he sure went around those rocks full speed until I caught her horse and saved the girl from maybe getting dragged or worse.

Marshal Hooker staged over four hundred exhibitions in two and a half years in the midwest. "Being fast is very important, but being accurate is far more important."

Once while in Raton, New Mexico, I was picked up for first degree murder. Stayed in jail awhile upstairs above the living quarters. They told me they were preparing to hang me when the real murderer was caught!

I went to work for a short while making hay on the Sheriff Black's ranch in Black Canyon. He wanted to make me foreman of the place, but the ranch was snowed in each winter for days and I didn't want that kind of a cold spell. While I was there the last wild buffalo from the old wild herds came down from the mountains. People went crazy! There were car loads of hunters with guns sticking out like a pin cushion, everyone wanting to kill that last poor old feeble buffalo. Also while I was there on Mr. Black's ranch, a bunch of ranchers went after a bunch of cattle rustlers. I liked the chase but didn't want any part of pulling the rope.

Not too far from here was a ranch, and at the roundup, two fellows had a bad feeling for each other. One day Jeff Woods hit Royal Ikie over the head with a neck yoke, and knocked him out. Ikie never said a word about it. But soon, on a cold morning, real early, Ikie got up and saddled his cow pony; he cautiously slipped a noose over Jeff Wood's feet under the blankets. The ground was frozen and a skim of ice was on the buffalo wallows, which were full of water. Letting out a rebel yell, Ikie spurred his horse and dragged Woods out from under his blankets, across the prairie, and through the buffalo wallows and frozen ground. He nearly killed the man. He dragged him back to camp, pitched his lariat off, went to the cattle herd and as far as I know that settled it.

I know of one man being shot while shaking hands to be friends. The other man was left handed and had his pistol on his left side. He shook hands with his right hand, holding on to the other man's hand, drew his gun and shot him in the stomach. The poor fellow lay on his back, his heels drumming on the ground until he died. Then another shot from across the street and the first man just crossed his legs and slid down the building wall into a sitting position and just sat there dead. I tell these things to let you know how it was when I was out there, and hope they are taken as I mean them to be. I know these things are not pleasant, but we have the same kind of people today who do much worse.

One time I was in Old Mexico and got into trouble. A pretty young Mexican girl got mad because I would not go with her to her crib. She raised a real fuss – it was in a saloon – and a huge Mexican cop was there. I thought for awhile this might be where my experiences could end! I got out and hired another Mexican to take me back to the border where I could cross over into the United States. After awhile I realized he was taking me farther into Mexico. Then we had trouble. Before I went across into Mexico, I hid what money I had, so when this fellow saw I had very little cash, he reluctantly took me north so I could find my way back home.

While a policeman, I confronted a young man who had two revolvers strapped on. The assistant chief of police said, "What shall we do?" I said, "Stand aside, and I'll get his guns." He came out of the pool hall where he had been letting off some steam and was drunk – he was celebrating. I stopped him and said, "It's against the law for you to wear those guns; take them off and hand them to Casey." I thought if I pulled my gun that he might react, so I just waited. I knew I could beat him to the draw. We just looked each other in the eye for a spell, then he unbuckled his guns and handed them over.

I remember one time as I was driving into Carthage on a cold wet day. I picked up a young man in Webb City; when we reached Carthage he told me to drive on north. He had on an overcoat with a gun in his pocket; I could see he would not hesitate to kill, so I refused to continue driving. As the traffic light turned green, many cars kept honking for me to drive on; I would not budge. He got excited, jumped out, and headed north. By the time I returned with my gun he was gone. He got to Jasper and was jailed for disturbing the peace in a restaurant. In the jail he locked up the officer and escaped northward. He was the Cook boy who left a trail of blood and death across the country. The pictures of the Mosser family he murdered, and whose bodies he dumped into a mine shaft at Joplin were taken by my brother Lee who worked for the *Carthage Evening Press*. I guess I would have been shot like so many other of his victims if I had driven him north. I would have been the first victim!

Another time I threw a man out of a hotel, at the manager's request. This fellow had recently killed a local man with his 45 automatic. He ran for his pickup truck saying he had something that would take care of me. When he came out with his gun I was standing only a few feet away, gun still in my holster. He was surprised and dropped his gun. He said he would get me

Marshal and George Earp — first cousin of Wyatt Earp.

later. He tried several times to get the best of me, but finally had to give it up. The gun I was wearing was a 45 double action Army Colt-1878 model — serial no. 41024, now owned by David Hall, Wood River, Illinois. The old Colt I carried in Arizona was a single action Army Colt 45-43/4 inch barrel — serial no. 218050, now belonging to my nephew, Eddie Hooker, Joplin. I got this 45 Colt from Harry Rogers, sheriff of Jasper County, Missouri. The one I carried at Silver Dollar City as a deputy sheriff for six years was a 45 Colt single action Army made in 1901, serial no. 193917 now owned by Steve Shedd. Dale Holly, Caney, Kansas, owns the 41 Remington Derringer I carried so long. If each of these guns could talk, they would surely tell some tall, exciting tales of danger.

Well, I remember one very cold night a bunch of fellows from the jungle camp crowded into a boxcar to keep from freezing. Someone had gotten the packing from the wheel axles and we had a fire in the middle of the car floor. I always thought that was the biggest collection of real cutthroats I was ever with at one time. I kept my hand on my knife all the time!

Another time when I was deputy sheriff, a nice looking young man came up to me and said, "I have heard that you are a fast draw and I have come to kill you." He said he was a fast draw artist and could beat me to the draw. At first I thought he was joking, then I saw he was in earnest. Well, this was a pretty stupid thing for anyone to do. I told him I was not fast and he could surely beat me getting into action, but if I saw him with his guns on I would put him under arrest, that I would outlast him, and he wouldn't live to tell about it. He went to get his gun. I guess he had second thoughts about it; he never came back. I never thought much about things like that and wasn't concerned, but some things I recall get to me yet. Like one night in a dark room with a man who had a cocked 45 in my stomach, and I wouldn't shoot as I knew who he was — I just couldn't shoot. And one night I was lost in a blizzard not far from Flagstaff, Arizona, another night on the Mescalero Apache Indian Reservation, and another night I almost drowned in the Missouri River in the winter time. I can still hear the pitiful cries of a female crying from a mine pit while shots were pumped into her to silence her.

One time I was living alone and was cut real bad. I was real sick and went home to bed. I woke up in the night and the bed around my face was soaked in blood and a puddle of blood was on the floor. I had to tough it out alone.

When a Civil War musket blew up with me in Noel, Missouri, filling my face with burning powder and steel, I was a bloody mess. It put a woman who was standing 30 feet away in the hospital. I still get powder and steel from my face, and only a few months ago, I had to have a piece of something cut out of my left temple.

Guard duty was one thing I liked. I guarded the Valley National Bank in Casa Grande when one wall was torn out for replacement of the adobe wall. I also guarded a quarter million dollar diamond shipment on display at Edmiston's store in Carthage.

You never know what is in a man's mind. I stayed all night with a very rich man in Kansas. He was a wealthy politician. He told me his life's dream was to be a shot gun guard on a stage coach. Better mention another thing that happened on the Kansas-Colorado corner. A bunch of boys were shooting cap and ball revolvers at each other, for fun, from the windows and doors of the old bunk house and the new bunk house one Sunday while the boss was away. The black powder guns were slower than the modern ones, and if you were fast enough and lucky, you could dodge when you saw smoke coming at you. One young fellow looked out the window just in time to catch a soft lead ball in the forehead. The cowboys took all of his belongings and wrapped him in a tarp, and dropped everything into a deep crack up in one of the canyons on the ranch. They told the boss the boy had decided to go home and had ridden out.

People do a lot of things they wish they hadn't. I found out, when I went to make all my wrongs right, that it wasn't easy. Like the Model T I took from a man in El Dorado, Kansas, and many other things. I suspect a lot of people feel sorry and the same way. Sometimes we don't do things in the order of their importance. And some things seem important that aren't; if we could have all our wishes, they could do us more harm than good.

An outlaw's money isn't a lasting thing. Gale Earp told me that George Earp once took Belle Starr, the Carthage girl outlaw, from Kansas City to Fort Smith, Arkansas, horseback to Hanging Judge Parker's court. She finally ended up by being shot in the back with a shot gun. It just didn't pay. Then there were the two boys who shot their friend while he was asleep in their hideout. They put him in a hack and started to town to collect the reward. On the way, the friend came to, and begged them to help him. They stopped the vehicle and shot him again. You can name them by the hundreds; while some escape and live, in the end the outlaw is always wrong and hurts innocent people.

Henry Starr, a really likeable and brave man, said to have robbed more banks than the James, Youngers, and Daltons put together, finally did it once too often. I have his cartridge belt he had on when he was shot in the bank in Harrison, Arkansas, in November, 1921, putting other people's money into a bag. I got the belt from the son of a man who took it off Starr in the bank. It is still full of 44-40 cartridges that Henry Starr put there. I have it from one of his friends who was in on the robbery, that they intended to rob another bank when they came to town. After Henry was shot, the boys drove south out of town toward Arkansas. They left the car they had on a bridge and got into another car hidden there. They then drove back through Harrison and on north. One of my friends loaned this man a revolver, that he used on a law officer and was killed himself in the fight.

A sad thing — a young man who was killed in front of the house where I lived in Oklahoma, shot with a shotgun and his heart blown out his back, ran several yards towards his home, leaving a trail of blood, before he died. One trip I made to California I was warned not to sleep in my car on the desert, as there were a lot of people being held up and killed. I was driving at night and got real sleepy, so I pulled out on the desert a ways. I was sleeping in the front seat, the old trusty 45 I carried in Casa Grande in my hand. I awakened suddenly and could hear someone fumbling with the car door. I threw the door open, jumped out and stuck my 45 in a man's face. He never said a word and I didn't either; slowly he backed up and got into a car that had rolled up behind me. Then another car behind him started up, two loads of

Marshal Hooker while serving as deputy sheriff at Silver Dollar City, Missouri. "I lived in this log cabin six years and cooked on the fireplace."

them trying to take another poor victim. Both cars backed up and they drove away. That was another time, among many, that my handgun saved my life. Sometimes you are not so prepared to defend yourself. I have stood with the bullets cutting tree limbs around me like hail, dozens of bullets. What about hiding on a ledge in the dark, a posse all around and a rider comes within arm's length, his horse snorting and trying to get away and it's too dark for the man to see you? Could that have been me?

For sure, when old Tom Golden, the cowboy from Kenna, New Mexico, stuck his big sixshooter in my middle it was bad enough, but when the boys who were with me all ran, that made it more so. Do you know what it is like to see dust flying from a man's clothes every time a bullet hits? I have seen it and it is not a very pleasant sight.

One time I took a marshal's job for a short time while the regular marshal took a vacation. Two fellows beat a man to death on the corner of the square. I was ready for them but they never came for me. At one place there was a dope ring and a lot of school kids were taking it. One boy got out on the highway and got in the wrong lane. I finally got him and he went into the Army to get out of his trouble. I tried to arrest a fellow in his home one time and it resulted in wrecking the inside of his place — a real shambles. Another time I tried to arrest a young fellow who had committed a crime. He was in a restaurant and as I went in the front door he went out the back. I followed him and as he ran down the alley in the dark, I got a bead on his back and he wouldn't stop, so I let him go but he came in the next morning. At one place I had a nice young heifer stolen. I was riding a pinto stallion hunting her. I found a place where they were getting ready to load cattle for shipping. Two men were there but said nothing as I rode up. I went among the cattle and saw my heifer with my cross H brand on her hip. I roped her and took her out of the pen. There was a lot of cattle rustling going on and most of these men were pretty mean. I expected trouble and was ready; maybe that's the reason I didn't have any.

The other day I went to Copan, Oklahoma, and took some pictures in front of the bank I was going to rob so long ago. It is closed now, and a lot of memories and things have happened since those days that seem so far in the past. But believe me, I wouldn't want to rob it today with Marshal Floyd Shell in town! Sometimes it seems like only a few days ago! What hurts is that people I knew are almost all gone. I walked the streets there, as in other places, looking for my friends, or those I rode with and they are no more, as I soon will be.

Just a word about shooting on a lighter note. I had heard about people going down the street shooting "just for the fun of it." I thought that I would like to try it, so I did; but that was the only time I was that foolish. People sure hunt for cover fast! The only thing wrong with that is that you might find someone that doesn't take kindly to it; then you've got troubles. After a display like that it would be too embarrassing to back down, so what are you going to do? It's a lot smarter not to do it in the first place.

At Gold's Store in Lincoln, Nebraska, I shot gas filled balloons during the day in front of a large crowd, and never missed one all day long with my 45. I fanned an egg sized rock from a waist high log. One chip big enough to see went flying to my right, and I whirled and fanned a quick shot and pulverized it, too.

At the Connor Hotel in Joplin, Missouri, at a meeting of the ROTC top brass, I was the entertainer for the night. Among other things I shot saucers out of the hand of my nephew, Lorie Hooker, with my old single action Colt.

At Silver Dollar City, while I was marshal there, a man followed me around making fun of me and calling me Wyatt Earp — he was trying to show off to impress three nice young ladies with him, only they were embarrassed. Finally I got tired of him; I told him to throw his hat in the air, a beautiful straw hat. This pleased him and with a flourish, he threw his hat in the air. I drew my 45 and blew the middle out of it.

Another time a man put a balloon on his head and said for me to shoot it off. I did — the balloon burst, and the man nearly had a heart attack. He was real quiet the rest of the evening. My son has held a small roll of paper in his mouth and I have shot it out a little at a time until I marked his front teeth. At an outdoor exhibition, I shot across the road at a playing card that was fastened to a tree. I drew and fanned five shots as fast as I could make the gun work and all five shots went well within the card. At another time, I fired into a block of wood, aiming, split the wood and had one piece of lead fastened together. I could throw two cups into the air, pull two guns and break them both. While a guest of the fast draw club, I shot a jackrabbit at quite a distance with a seven inch barrel 45 Colt single action and got him in the eye. A friend of mine, Tony Desmuck of Wichita, put a small bottle in a tree about 71 yards away and fast drew his single action and blew it to pieces. There are quite a few fast shots. I can't do these things any more; one hand went through a table saw; a bullet from a Colt got my left trigger finger, and my reactions are not so good, nor are my eyes any more.

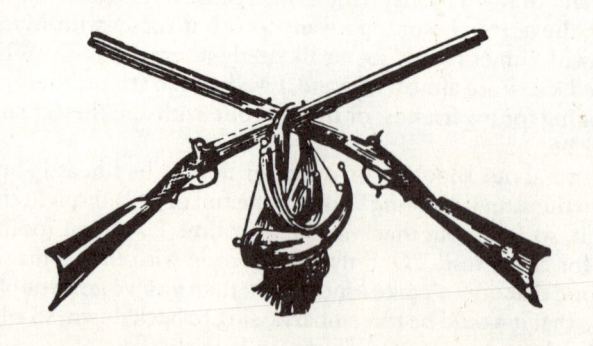

Chapter IX

IT had always been my dream to walk the Santa Fe Trail. This dream was realized in 1958 when a garment factory agreed to sponsor me in this adventure. It was a big advertising campaign for their work clothes and western wear. My beautiful embroidered shirts carried their advertisement; they also gave me contacts along the way, and many people kindly helped me on this adventure. My good friend and adviser, Dick Ferguson, encouraged and helped me to make the necessary connections to make my trip possible and pleasant.

The earliest roads in America were trails made by the Indians; they were no more than just paths through the wilderness that were passable by foot or horseback but not for wagons or stagecoaches. In order for settlers to move their families and household wares, roads had to be built. This was an arduous task, trees had to be cut down and paths cleared through trackless forests and over seas of mud. Streams could only be crossed in shallow places so roads had to be planned with this in mind.

The roads were crude, holes filled with brush and rocks where trees had been removed; ruts and bumps made it difficult for wagons to travel especially in wet weather when the roads were muddy. The Santa Fe Trail was one of the longest commercial routes before railroads were built. It extended 780 miles from Independence, Missouri to Santa Fe, New Mexico. It could be made in less time if the Cimarron short cut was used, but this pass was unsafe.

In 1821, Captain William Becknell left Arrow Rock, Missouri with a pack train loaded with goods which he had hopes of selling for a great profit to settlers in New Mexico. At that time, it was a part of Old Mexico; when he returned with his mules loaded with packs of silver the news spread like wildfire. It soon became a popular trade route; strings of caravans traversed the dusty prairies to New Mexico and returned with Mexican money and goods. It was highly remunerative but extremely dangerous. Indians lurked in thickets and gulches waiting to attack; even the Mexican Military officials' attitudes were uncertain. The white animal bones covered the prairies and many traders' scalps decorated the Comanche wigwams. But trade pushed on; in 1846 during the Mexican-American War, a column of Missouri

Marshal Hooker holding the Boone rifle which he carried with him, ready to begin the Santa Fe Trail walk in 1958.

soldiers followed the trail and conquered New Mexico from the enemy and raised our flag. Trade increased to a greater degree, but the old trail was deserted after the railroads came into use.

I started my trek on May 3, 1958, by leaving for Lamy, New Mexico and then taking a bus to Santa Fe. I made the trip in reverse because I wanted to get over the hottest and driest parts before it got hotter and drier, as I used the dry and dangerous Cimarron cutoff. I carried a five pound pack and my muzzle loading rifle. I also carried a letter from Natalie Smith Buck, Secretary of State of New Mexico to Governor James Blair, Jr., of Missouri.

It was truly a rugged trail. About a week out of Santa Fe my feet swelled and caused me great discomfort. I was also very tired. I took only one pound of dried prunes along; I was following the wagon trail and slept out in the open without blankets. However, I never thought about giving up!

Most of the trip I tramped through rain and storms which made the trip more laborious. I felt that this was much more rugged for me than for the pioneers for they at least had their covered wagons to get into out of the weather. Many people think of the desert as just dry, sandy expanses of land, but it really has a beauty all its own. When one looks across a sunbaked mesa and the desert of white gypsum up to the snow capped mountains in the distance, one feels a sense of quiet peace in such vastness. I felt very removed from the outer world as I trudged along. It was wonderful to breathe the unpolluted air, although the altitude was high (about 1½ miles)

The Santa Fe Trail about nine miles out of Dodge City, Kansas.

which gave me some difficulty in breathing sometimes; I had to stop and rest more often.

Had it not been for the sleet storms and rains I encountered I would have enjoyed the trip more, but I slept out on the prairie on the cold wet ground and listened to the coyotes yowling their mournful cries. I drank the cold water from the buffalo wallows — the sweetest water I ever drank. The soles of my feet blistered and peeled off causing me great pain; I sat on the cold ground and soaked my feet in those cold buffalo wallows until all feeling was gone, then I continued to hobble on.

I carried an old flint lock rifle which had a hand-hammered barrel; it was made by Elisa Buell around 1775. The length was 5 ft. 2 in. and it weighed 10½ pounds. It shot a .457 ball. This rifle was purchased from Daniel Boone by Byron Ash's grandfather, who lived on the banks of the Ohio River. On his long trips Boone often stopped at the Ash's place to rest. The rifle was kept in the Ash family until it was given to me in 1946. It is still very accurate and in good shooting condition.

In many places the old wagon ruts were very plain; these were the times when I related to the frontiersmen I had read about all my life. I visualized the hardships and dangers they must have encountered along this very trail I was following.

I passed the old Fort Union (seven miles from the highway) which for many years was the only place between Watrous, New Mexico and Missouri where a person could sleep in a bed. I got a room to sleep in at Watrous, but it was so noisy and stunk so from the beer joint below that I went out and slept on the ground.

My feet hurt me and I was becoming discouraged when suddenly a white pigeon flew close to me and settled in front of me a few feet away. I didn't think much about it until it repeated its actions for a long distance; it seemed to encourage me to continue on in faith. In this locality an early mountain man reported seeing 65 grizzly bears at sunset at one time — my worst enemy was Brahma cattle! I came to a large lake but the water was too dirty to drink. The wind was high and the small waves crested into the sandy shore line; I soaked my feet in its icy waters. Farther down the road I passed a windmill and pond where I drank my fill of clear fresh water and filled my canteen. When I arrived, two beautiful white geese rose gracefully from the pond and drifted off into somewhere. It began to rain and storm, and I took cover under a large ledge and munched on some prunes. This is really roughing it.

Some of the towns I passed through were terribly filthy, especially those inhabited by the Mexicans. When I reached Springer, New Mexico on May 11, I stayed all night at a hotel to take care of my feet. I soaked my feet in water which seemed to relieve them a great deal. I rested there until noon the next day. I had intended to hit the road, but some city officials asked me to speak at the Chamber of Commerce meeting and also at the high school. Consequently, I spent another night at the hotel, which really was better for my sore feet. A very gracious woman washed and ironed my clothes.

The next day it rained and hailed but I walked along in the inclement weather, jackrabbits playing on both sides of the road. I put the butt of

Boone's rifle on a rattle snake's head and twisted off his rattlers and brought them to my nephew in Joplin.

Taylor Springs is just a blink-of-the-eye type of town, but is located in a beautiful deep valley. The snow peaked mountains lay behind me. Often times people drove by as I walked along the highway, stopped and invited me to ride but I declined. West of Abbot, New Mexico, I spied a large herd of antelopes standing so close I could have easily shot them with Boone's rifle. Northeast of Abbot I found the old Santa Fe Trail; it was at least four feet deep and 150 feet across.

Some days I didn't walk as far as other days; sometimes it was because my feet were still tender and sometimes because of bad weather. Some of the towns had been notified of my project and people greeted me with great hospitality. Often times I visited schools and civic organizations and talked to them about my trip and Boone's gun. They enjoyed my shooting and tales of many other experiences.

At Clayton, New Mexico, two citizens took me up in their airplane so that I could see the trail from the air. I saw it for miles in either direction and was amazed at the view; in some places it was a mile wide. I could see the water holes and campsites — foundations of old buildings that were crumbling along the trail. A herd of antelope grazed nonchalantly by a water hole. The trail was clearly visible from the air. I noticed a farm house had been built in the middle of the trail. Some of the ranchers were using the old trail to get to other places. This was cattle country — the land of big hats, blue jeans, and cowboy boots.

The next day I enjoyed a beautiful walk as the sun rose in the clear sky. At noon I ate a few prunes by the side of the road on the Texas and New Mexico boundary, known as Clark boundary 1859. About seven miles this side of Felt, Oklahoma, a carload of people stopped to chat with me and gave me a banana that sure did taste good.

I spent the night on a sand bar on the north bank of the Beaver River. This is NO MAN'S LAND, a strip of Oklahoma. The coyotes were yelping and wailing their lamenting songs as a soft cool breeze brushed the tall grasses; the night grew colder and I had very little sleep. I finally gave up and started walking again, arriving in Boise City, Oklahoma at three o'clock in the morning; this covered 55 miles in one stretch of walk. I was so tired and sore that I took a room in a run down hotel that had no conveniences — $1.79 for the room. This city was a dusty, dirty western town. It was celebrating its 50th year in local history of the Santa Fe Trail, outlaws, etc. I struck out again in the cool of the morning to hit the trail; saw several beautiful pheasants. By noon it had grown so hot it was almost unbearable. I stopped in Keyes to eat some lunch and get a cool drink. There I met some men who told me they had found some old guns and knives in some deserted camps one mile east of town. I only trudged 30 miles this day because of the heat.

One time I took shelter under a large outcropping to rest from the searing sun; my water was low, but a man passing by on a tractor filled my canteen. Here the fields were cultivated and there were no buffalo wallows. Continuing down the road I arrived at a small place named Sturges, which had only a farm house as its landmark. The heavens opened up and the rain and hail

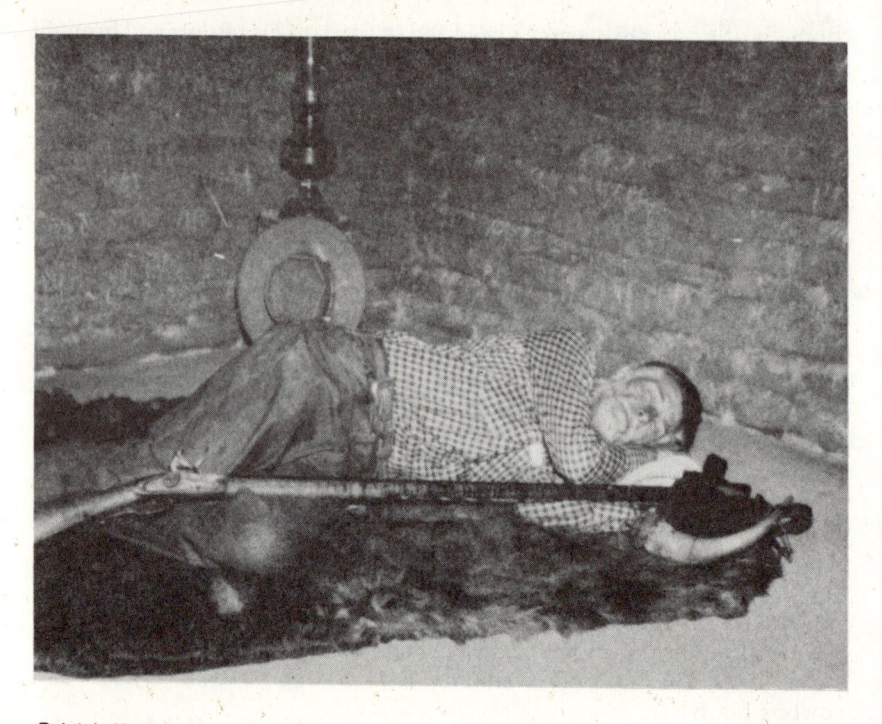

Ralph L. Hooker spent the night in this adobe house in Hillsboro, Kansas in 1958 on the Santa Fe Trail walk.

pelted down. The rancher in the farm house offered me a night's lodging in an old sod house. It was very dirty but it was better than the ground after the rain. The bed was so dirty and the rats rummaged around so that I could not sleep much.

I left early the next morning and reached Elkhart, Kansas. I had lived almost exclusively on prunes and had lost 25 pounds. When I was offered food I had to eat sparingly as my stomach had shrunk and I would get very sick as I couldn't keep the food down. I met some very friendly people here; the sheriff Leroy Taylor took me out to Point of Rocks, an interesting place about 12 miles north of Elkhart.

The next day as I started out again the sky was cloudy and the morning cool; about eight miles out of town a rancher stopped and offered me a ride which I refused. I made 33 miles that day and arrived in Hugoton where I was warmly welcomed by some of the civic leaders — the sheriff Code Hall, city police, and some of the dealers of the western wear I was advertising. Code Hall and his deputies, Merle Peachy and Wayne Nordick, took me back to Point of Rocks the next day. This Point of Rocks was where the pioneers of the Santa Fe Trail got up high on the point to watch both ways on the trail for Indians and outlaws. There was a famous ranch at the foot of the rocks in those days, but a flood washed away the entire ranch and took the lives of many people. The old well that furnished the water for the ranch had caved in and now existed as a huge hole. Here the rattle snakes denned up, bred and came out; people went out there to hunt rattlers because there were thousands of them. On the day we were there it was cold and cloudy and this kind of weather was not inviting to the snakes to leave their holes. I wanted to get one so badly to prepare and eat, for I had always heard it was such a good delicacy. The people came out from town with several cans of gasoline and coal oil and poured it into the well and threw a match in. It boiled up for several hundred feet around and cooked the snakes until it smelled like something cooking in a kitchen. They did this once a year because so many ranchers and horses were bitten by rattlesnakes. It killed thousands of them.

I was standing in a place where the hill was honeycombed with small caves — the kind one has to get down and crawl into. A week before I got there some boys were hunting around this very area and found a petrified Indian woman in perfect condition. Just before I got there they had taken her out and to a museum. It seems strange that with all the thousands of people on the Sante Fe Trail, the many cowboys and tourists, this woman was in the cave only a few feet from the mouth of the opening. She still had clothing on that was woven on the ancient looms out of mountain sheep hair. The clothing was not in perfect condition, but there was enough left of it to cover her body.

The Jedediah Smith marker north of Hugoton, Kansas where Smith was killed by Commanche Indians while searching for water near the Cimarron River.

From the Point of Rocks we went down on the Cimarron River by a place called Wagon Bed Springs. This was where Jedediah Smith, the mountain man, was killed by Comanches while hunting for water. No one knew exactly where he was killed, but knew within a few hundred yards and placed a monument there. A group of traders had come into Santa Fe with his rifle and told how they had talked with the Comanches, who told them how they killed him and left him there. This place was called Wagon Bed Springs because in the early days it was muddy and swampy around it. One day some people came from Ulysses, Kansas and buried a Weber Wagon bed around the springs so they could dip water from it and water their horses and stock. George Earp, Wyatt's first cousin, was one of the people who helped put the wagon bed around the springs. One of the people who came out and talked with us was a descendant of some of the people who were with George Earp at the time. I stayed here for three days. Friends showed me various places of interest along the Santa Fe Trail in the area.

From here I went north of the trail to Lakin, Kansas and was the guest of the famous Buddy Heaton, radio and movie star. This was beautiful wheat country — the wheat growing as high as my chin. The weather was terribly hot and there was no shade to get relief. All along the trail the people were most kind to me. A few times I spent the nights in their homes and ate delicious meals. Some of them washed my shirts, which really made me feel better to start back traveling. One night I stopped at a deserted cowboy line shack; I was so tired I almost dropped in my tracks. There was no furniture and it was close to falling in, but it was cover for the night. I sat down against a wall and drew up my legs. I put Boone's rifle between my feet and wrapped my arms around it and slept. During the night the rats smelled the grease in the grease hole where Daniel Boone had used grease on the patchings. Those rats chewed the rim in this old maple wood by smelling that grease of so long ago.

I finally arrived in Cimarron, Kansas, which is supposed to be the half way mark on the Santa Fe Trail to Independence. Bullet marks still show on some buildings where Bat Masterson and Bill Tilgham and others had this county seat war.

By the time I reached Dodge City, my left ankle was swollen and hard and very sore. My right big toe was black and throbbing furiously; a doctor wanted to put me in the hospital. I had made poor time that day because of these ailments. Some city officials and the sheriff brought me to the Dodge House Hotel where I took a good bath and had a good night's sleep. The next day I felt better and visited around Dodge City. I had an interview on their radio station; I walked past Boot Hill. As I passed the jail a man looked through the window and called, "Hi, Wyatt!" I spoke at the Lions Club luncheon and later the Mayor of Dodge City presented me with a Marshal Commission of Dodge City. I left Dodge about 4:30 in the morning and took my time walking the trail. My left leg was giving me trouble again, so I decided to take it easy and rest more often. Along the way many people were interested in my Boone rifle. It seemed to impress greatly — young and old alike — when I fired the rifle for them. At Fort Larned I shot Boone's rifle from the loop holes that Hickok, Custer, and Buffalo Bill had used fighting Indians.

Ralph L. Hooker accepting commission as Honorary Marshal of Dodge City, Kansas, from Mayor N.O. Reese, during his Santa Fe Trail crossing.

G. G. Robbins, president of the Larned, Kansas Chamber of Commerce and Walter Hembrow, President of the US-56 Highway Association visit with Ralph L. Hooker at the Pawnee Rock monument in Kansas.

Pawnee Rock had a Boy Scout troup dressed as Indians, who captured me as I walked into town. I walked on to Great Bend, Kansas following the Trail far away from the highway; I walked as far as I could on the trail until it veered back to the highway. As I got to the road there were two rough, burly looking boys waiting for me. I had been on many talk shows on TV and radio so people kept up with my itinerary and knew where I'd be at certain times after I got into Kansas. I had been a police officer for enough years to know what these two fellows had in mind; when I got there I knew they intended to rob me. I took out my bowie knife to protect myself. Both of them turned and made for their car and left. The rain had turned the fields into mud and after walking all day in that, great clumps of mud clung to my shoes and it was hard walking. Soon my legs felt almost paralyzed. I had staggered up to the road and seen those two bullies leering at me; I breathed a sigh of relief that I didn't have to fight them with the muddy shoes handicapping me. In Baldwin I was made a deputy sheriff and given the badge worn by a great old time lawman, Buck Jones.

In Galva, Kansas, in a cafe a man put up a bet that I could hit an iron plug on a telephone pole. This was a rich farming community composed mostly of the Amish people. At noon they came into this cafe for lunch; the men wore their black hats and the women their little bonnets. They are a very frugal people. This man was bound and determined that I show off my marksmanship. I tried to explain to him that I was tired and was sure I couldn't even hit the pole, let alone the small marker on it, but he laughed and said, "There are only two kinds of people from Missouri, and those are the good ones and the bad ones. The good ones are all squirrel hunters. They can shoot their rifles and the rest don't matter!" Then he turned to his customers and said, "You just watch this man shoot that rifle." I pleaded with him, asking him not to do this to me, for I was so tired and shaky and weak, I didn't think I could hit anything. "Aw, no, I don't believe that. I think you can do it," he said, ignoring my pleas. He began passing the hat around for the bet money. I got another bright idea, so said, "I can't shoot here anyhow; I'm in the city. You surely have an ordinance against shooting within the city limits." He said, "All right. The county line is right out here in the middle of the road, so you can get on the other side of this road and you can shoot. You don't have any excuse." I gave up! I saw he was determined so went out across the road and took up my position to sight across to the pole which was about a hundred yards away. The county or some official employee had put an aluminum marker for some identification of that area. I hunched down on one foot and rested my arm and my gun on my knee, took careful aim and prayed that I would at least hit the post. When we went to look at the target, after I shot, it looked as though soft lead had been poured over it. It was a perfect hit! I was really proud of it, and brought the plug home to put among my souvenirs. This man stuffed the money from his hat into my pockets. One of the men took me east of town to his birthplace on the Trail and showed me the deep wagon ruts. He told me that there used to be a town there called Empire, and a road which left from there was named The Fayetteville Arkansas Military Road; however, there is no sign of the road or the town today.

In Canton, Kansas I met a man, Vernon Nikkel, who became one of my best friends. He met me on the trail outside of town and took me home with him for the night. My feet were bleeding badly and he doctored them. It was through him and his friends that arrangements were made for me to shoot a buffalo on the Maxwell State Game Reserve. We went out to the prairie that was virgin land covered with prairie hay. The buffalo couldn't be found the first day. The next morning we came across the herd just as the sun was coming up; they stood up and stretched, their tails curling over their backs just as cattle do when they get up. There was one cow that had stopped

First buffalo killed with Boone rifle at Maxwell Game Reserve near Hesston, Kansas.

having calves; the caretaker pointed out the dry cow with the crooked horn that I was to kill. We circled for awhile until I could get a good shot at her. A curious crowd gathered with movie cameras, etc. They didn't think the Boone rifle could kill a buffalo, so they had back up guns to kill her in case my rifle couldn't. But I hit her in the forehead. One of the rangers jumped off the truck and put a chain around her neck and used a winch to lift her up. The other buffaloes began milling around trying to get to her so we made for the fence. The buffaloes began fighting and following us. We took the 1250 pound cow to Canton to be skinned. They gave me the head and the hide. It was a great experience. I later returned to Canton when the buffalo was barbecued and eaten. I was in the parade and given a key to the city.

Most of the places had the welcome mat out for me, but some places — including the dealers of the merchandise I was advertising — weren't interested in my venture. Marion, Kansas went all out to make me feel welcome; this friendly town hung banners across the streets with WELCOME inscribed across. They lodged me, dined me, and showed keen interest in my Boone rifle and my experiences. In these cordial towns I gave away many pictures of myself and my rifle, signed many autographs, appeared on their radio and television stations, and talked to schools and other groups.

They prepared a great feast for me in Council Grove. During the last leg of my Santa Fe Trail journey, as I crossed Kansas City and headed for Independence, Missouri, I was provided with a police escort complete with flashing red lights and sirens. A lavish dinner had been set up and was waiting for me at the new Union Station on Wyandotte Street. Great crowds came to see me; I signed many autographs, met many celebrities and posed for several television cameras. A cavalcade of cars accompanied me to Independence, including police escorts. They wanted me to ride but I was determined to finish the trip walking it. It was difficult for them to slow down to my walking speed. It was a fifteen mile trip to the "finish line."

My feet had healed up pretty well but on this walk they broke open again and when I reached Independence my socks were soaked with blood. I was truly tired when I walked into Kansas City, but now it was really grueling because of the pressure of the crowds and all the activities. I was therefore so grateful to my friend, Richard Ferguson, the representative of the company that sponsored this trip, for meeting me in Independence and getting me a nice clean room to rest in. That evening we went into the blue room of this lovely motel to have our dinner. It was full of elite people who were dining, drinking, and enjoying soft music. When I walked in with my rifle, my trail-worn clothes, long beard and hair, they began to laugh and joke at me. I was too tired to care; our meal was delicious. Then the news came on the television set and showed some of the different places along the trail where I had been. The room grew deathly quiet when they realized they had made fun of me, and I was the one the film was all about. At the end of the film the lights were turned on and everybody gave me a standing ovation. Several came to me and apologized for their rudeness.

The next day a big parade was planned and this time I rode. The highlight of it all was the dinner which ex-President Truman arranged for me. A few days before I arrived a half-wit had taken a shot at Mr. Truman, planning to assassinate him, so they searched everyone who entered the dining hall, except me. I had a pistol in my pocket that I had carried on my trip. I sat across from Mr. Truman and could have very easily killed him, had I entertained such a henious thought. I would have quickly defended him rather than hurt him. That episode proves what possibilities can arise. He personally conducted me through the Truman Memorial Library and his office. I spent some sixty minutes with this great man talking about the Trail and the history of the Old West. His grandfather had gone west on the Santa Fe Trail.

Independence is recognized as the Queen City of the Trails. I was presented the gold key to the city. My adventures ended July 15, 1958 — a total of 63 days.

I have reflected upon the benefits of this walk from time to time. I'm sure I have acquired a deeper sense of understanding and appreciation of my heritage as I walked in the foot prints of great frontiersmen. I remembered

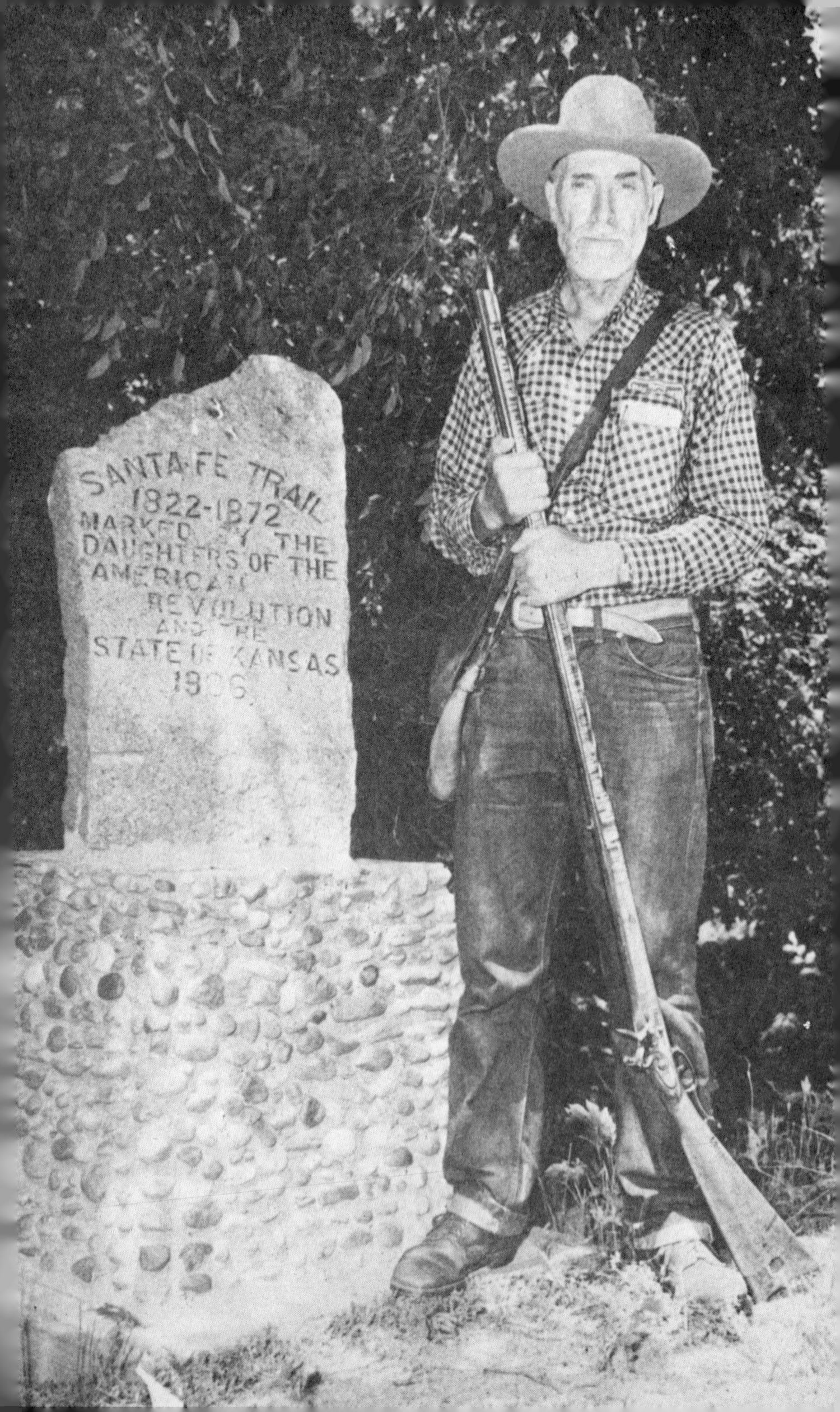

the time I fired the Boone rifle through the old port holes of Fort Larned, Kansas where Custer, Hickok, Cody, and other frontiersmen had fought off the Indians. The Fort had been restored, but this part had never been changed. People who were restoring the Fort were quite elated at having Boone's rifle shot through the port-holes.

Trudging along by myself I recalled many incidents that my history books had revealed to me about those days. Sometimes I felt I could almost hear those wagon wheels crunching along behind me in the quiet of the day. Or the pounding hooves of Felix Aubry's horse when he covered the entire length of the trail in a little more than five days using several horses, and he had to be cut from the saddle as he had tied himself in to keep from falling out, for fear he would go to sleep. I remember being told that when so many were traveling the trail, the camp fires could be seen in both directions until they faded out in the distance. Also one would never, at any one time, be out of sight of the graves, or see things that had been dumped from wagons too broken-down to travel on. People died and friends picked up remaining parties. The trail was lined with bleached bones and skeletons all along the way after one entered Kansas, especially after a few miles where Indians were still giving trouble. They had quit in Missouri. This last known and used trail, so far as I could find out, was traveled by a caravan of wagons that went for the same purpose as the original wayfarers — to get ground and live — in 1915. A group went west over the same trail all the way into New Mexico.

These momentous accounts of brave people made a great impact on my understanding of the roots of our freedom. It took great suffering, sacrifice, and vision. To feel the awesomeness of it all, one needs to walk in the footprints of destiny.

It is not easy. In one little town I fell from exhaustion and was too weak to get up. Two young men set me on my feet and I walked on. I think of the cold nights, severe storms, miles from any living soul, the snakes, starvation, and black nights where I could know no direction and I couldn't sleep from the cold. I would lie down on the cold, cold ground to rest and point my rifle barrel in the direction I wanted to go when I got up, then follow the ruts by feeling the way with my feet. I had a wealth of pictures to show of this trip, but they were taken and destroyed by one I thought was a dear friend.

Chapter X

WHEN a man reaches his late 50's he should be considering slowing down his activities and relegating his thoughts toward the old rocking chair. At least, this had been told me by some of my venerable peers, but somehow I never gave my beckoning dotage much thought. I still had my yens and dreams as I had in my youth. I wasn't afraid to take a cold plunge into the future. To me, that is what life is all about. The year after my 780 mile walk on the Santa Fe Trail, I approached the same garment manufacturer who sponsored my walk, and members of the Appaloosa Horse Breeders Association, to sponsor me in riding the old Chisholm Trail.

I knew the Chisholm Trail was a 1040 mile expedition. I was much interested and eager to accomplish this itinerary and knew that an important extremity of my body needed some toughening up. I was never one who did a lot of sitting around. Be that as it may I was sure that I could cope with the situation as I did with my feet.

This excursion was quite alluring to my nephew, Merrill Hooker, Jr., who took a leave of absence from his work to join me. He was only twenty-one and had had no experience riding a horse. His eagerness was only youthful anticipation of adventure regardless of consequences. He didn't consider the effects behind the project.

Bob Hurt, owner of the Hurt Trailer works of Sarcoxie, Missouri, furnished my four-year-old Appaloosa stallion named War Cloud. Swede Tomlinson of Oklahoma City furnished my nephew with a twelve year old gelding called Turk. The horses were loaded into trailers and we took off for Kingsville, Texas, the beginning of the trail. Man has raised cattle since history was first written. Men of the old stone age were driven out by other races who brought in cattle. The Egyptian tombs attest to the use of oxen plowing and treading grain some 12,000 years ago. Christopher Columbus brought the first cattle to the Americas in 1493, according to history. As the pioneers moved westward they carried on cattle raising. The railroads later helped the ranchers transport their cattle to the eastern markets.

The Chisholm Trail was the old route over which Texas ranchers drove their cattle to the railroads in Kansas. The trail passed through Runge, Texas

Marshal Hooker on War Cloud during the 1048 mile Chisholm Trail ride in 1959.

to Helena, Montana and points north. We planned on following the trail as near as modern highways would permit us. We equipped ourselves with saddle-bags, ponchos, blanket rolls and canteens, thus prepared to stay any place. We were to test the durability of our western wear and the stamina of the horses. We kept records of mileage per day, cost and amount of feed, etc., for the benefit of the stockmen and breeders. We each carried a Colt 45 in open holster with cartridge belts.

We left Kingsville, Texas on May 2, 1959, on a grey, rainy morning. The air was warm and muggy but this didn't dampen our enthusiasm for the trip. "Sure am glad I toughened up a little in this saddle before we started," Merrill said confidently. "You mean that hour you rode around yesterday on Turk?" I asked. "Yep, that gave me the feel of the saddle and to get acquainted with Turk," he said patting his horse's neck convincingly. That evening we were invited by a Mexican tenant farmer to rest at his place; we watered and fed our horses. We were just getting settled down to sleep in the feed lot when the farmer's wife came out and told us to move on. We didn't understand her objections to our staying there for the night, but who can argue with a woman sputtering wildly in a language you couldn't even understand? We had already traveled 35 miles that day, but we saddled up and moved on. A mile farther north we found a deserted cotton gin and fixed ourselves a comfortable place to sleep on a nearby loading ramp. About three o'clock in the morning an owl inside began making weird noises, evidently having fallen out of his nest. After all, who wouldn't get upset when falling out of bed? The noise got worse as the wind came up and rattled the loose tin roof. Some restful night in the old gin!

The weather was cool and riding was pleasant. The horses seemed more rested as we rode down the road talking and planning. War Cloud suddenly jumped aside and Turk followed suit; there ahead of us lay two big rattlesnakes in the middle of the road. Rattlesnakes are good eating, but we left them behind for the road runners.

Outside of Skidmore, Texas we were permitted to stable and corral our horses while we slept in the granary. We left early the next morning and rode to Beeville. We used our big hats to carry water to our horses because some people refused to let us water them. In one town one of the men gave us a snake-kit because the rattlers were particularly bad in this area.

At Kennedy, Texas we enjoyed the great hospitality of the people; we had lunch with the Rotarian Group who were very interested in our venture. That afternoon it rained and grew hot; we were glad when we reached a pond to water our horses. I found that one can never understand the motives of a horse. As I was watering War Cloud at the pond, he suddenly decided to refresh himself more than just by a drink. He lay down in the water and rolled over, almost rolling me with him. His actions were so quick I was caught off guard. Turk followed my horse's lead — fell to the ground and tried to roll over with Merrill. I know it seemed a funny situation, but only the horses were laughing. War Cloud was in quite a bit of pain from saddle sores.

By the time we reached Temple, Texas, War Cloud had saddle sores on both sides. I contacted a veterinarian, who gave me some salve and also checked over the horses; they had lost some weight but otherwise were in good condition. Meantime, Merrill washed our clothes while I went shopping for some supplies.

Merrill kept complaining about his big white hat blowing off now and then and he had to stop and run after it. Every time it got wet it stretched until now it fit him around the ears. I asked him why he didn't tie it on with a piece of string. He had started out with a raw-hide chin strap, but every time something broke loose on the saddle he had to use a piece of it for patching and had used it all. Merrill was a good trail companion and we enjoyed each other's company very much. We rode through all kinds of weather and slept in all kinds of places. Merrill always preferred sleeping in the nude; he said it was warmer this way than sleeping in his wet clothes all night. Sometimes I would arise early and jerk the covers off him and yell, "Get up and beat your chest!" This provoked him; he'd shake his 45 at me and yell back, "Marshal, if you weren't my uncle I'd kill you." Even that smacked of old west jargon. I was glad he smiled after he said it.

As we neared Austin a jet bomber came in for a landing, passing so closely overhead that the horses were terrified. The noise and vibrations were terrible and the horses acted up. We stayed at the livestock auction barns there; traffic was so heavy in town that I asked for and received a police escort across the Colorado River Bridge.

About three miles south of Belton, Texas we were caught in a bad rainstorm accompanied by hard-hitting hail stones. In the old days, the cattle would probably have stampeded; I thought perhaps War Cloud would get some such idea but he seemed to be in control of the situation. The police located an old cowboy who stabled and fed our horses; a very hospitable gentleman housed us for the evening. We were wet, cold, and hungry. We dried our clothes by the fire in his fireplace.

In the beginning in south Texas, cowboys roped the wild Spanish longhorns and sewed their eyes together and bunched them in herds. The cowboys would then ride around them and sing, getting them used to human beings. They could smell water and drink and graze; by the time the eyes festered and the stitches fell out they could see again and were used to the men so that they could be driven down the trail. Hundreds of thousands of longhorns were driven east, west, and north. Jesse Chisholm, part Indian, drove a hack through the grass and trail drivers followed his tracks; the trail was named after him. He also had a trading post on the trail.

Early in May the prairie was covered with a beautiful carpet of wild flowers including Texas blue-bonnets, and luscious green grass. We ran into another cold rain which made traveling and sleeping miserable. On the south bank of the Brazos River we saw the rubble of a former wild rough town named Kimball, which had been established right on the trail. The last old timer who lived there used to sit on his porch evenings with a shotgun across his legs and he took the gun everywhere he went. In Fort Worth we were met by several riders at the Cowtown Posse Rodeo Grounds; they all showed us a wonderful time. The owner of the Justin Boot Company presented Merrill and me with two pairs of beautiful boots. We shipped our old ones home. Many pictures were taken and interviews given, also there was a great feed at the western restaurant.

Pursuing our trail, we rode through wild grass as high as the saddle horns. The horses walked at their own speed, filling up on the delicious grass. At Alvord, I bought a Winchester saddle gun from a former Texas Ranger. Merrill carried this rifle the remainder of the trip. Four miles north of Bowie, we spent the night in a persimmon grove. There was excellent wild hay that we cut into huge piles with our bowie knives for the horses. A car load of young men drove out to visit us and talk about our trip.

We crossed the Red River into Oklahoma; we were now over half way to our destination. In Addington, Oklahoma we turned the horses loose in the railroad shipping pens where the wild hay was abundant. Then we got the bed rolls ready for another night under the stars.

A little way south of Comanche, a traveling horse-shoer put four new shoes on Turk and new ones on War Cloud's front feet, resetting the ones on his hind feet. It was raining and cold when we crossed the Cimarron River. In the growing darkness traffic was getting heavier all the time. Now we were beginning to meet combines and their outfits on the road for the wheat harvest. At one point we began crossing a bridge and a large truck approached us; the driver seemed to understand our predicament and drove very slowly and quietly. (Maybe War Cloud was too tired to try anything rash.) I thanked God for giving us safe crossing for it could have ended up in quite a calamity. We were so grateful to find a place to bed down for the night as we were tired and hungry. I sympathized with War Cloud that

Marshal Hooker and Lori Hooker on 1040 mile Chisholm Trail — Kingsville, Texas to Abilene, Kansas.

evening as I turned him into a corral and fed him; he showed his appreciation for my concern by stepping on my right foot.

By the time we left Enid the weather had cleared and it looked like smooth-going into Abilene, however one can't depend on the good to last. North of Jefferson, Oklahoma catastrophe struck! As we were riding along I suddenly found myself standing on the ground with War Cloud under me, but with both hind legs in a hole up to his belly. It was an uncovered, unmarked water meter hole beside the roadway. I had no sooner left the saddle than War Cloud came out of the hole, cutting both legs, one severely, and tearing one shoe almost off the other foot. Merrill rode ahead to locate a veterinarian, but drew a blank. With War Cloud hobbling painfully along, we made our way to a ranch where we all rested and ate. Merrill rode ahead again while I walked with War Cloud who was in great pain and losing a considerable amount of blood. A veterinarian named Zeplensky was waiting for us when we arrived about dark. Had we not been in luck to find this doctor, our trail ride would have ended there. We stayed there two days to rest. After getting on the trail again, this doctor came out and treated War Cloud again.

Before arriving in Wichita we slept on the ground at a roadside park. It was a terribly cold night; in the morning I crossed the road to a small store and bought some bacon, eggs, and buns. The proprietor loaned me a skillet and two forks. Merrill and I had a good breakfast out in the open, having cooked it on a grill in the park.

It began to rain again as we rode into Wichita. For some reason Turk skittishly jumped and broke his stirrup leather. Merrill was thrown on his side but could not dismount because his spur was all hung up in his bed roll. However, he righted himself and we continued. We stayed in a motel on the outskirts of town where I cut grass for the horses. Merrill went into town to get the stirrup leather fixed. I sprayed the horses; War Cloud got his leg opened up again and it was bleeding badly.

On June 10 we rode into Abilene, Kansas, the end of our 40 day trail crossing of more than 1040 miles. Quite a crowd had been waiting for us at the Smoky Hill River bridge south of Abilene. We rode into old Abilene town and down Texas Street, where another crowd had gathered for the End of the Trail Ceremonies! We were asked to "shoot up the town" as in the old days, so we emptied our guns in the air as part of the celebration.

In my saddle bag I carried a letter from the chief of police of Carthage, Bill Loyd, to the chief of police in Abilene; a letter from Mayor Robert Eddy of Carthage to the mayor of Abilene; a letter from Sheriff Hickman of Jasper County, Missouri to the sheriff of Dickinson County, Kansas; and a letter from George Earp of Joplin, the only living cousin of Wyatt Earp, to the mayor of Abilene. The editor of the Abilene newspaper presented and read the certificate making me the first honorary marshal of old Abilene town, and Merrill the second honorary marshal. Later we received official badges authenticating this honor. There was a big parade for us through Abilene and out to the fair grounds where the horses were stabled for the night. We handed the reins of the horses to Bob Hurt, who came from Sarcoxie for the festivities. The Chisholm Trail crossing was officially completed!

War Cloud had lost 25 pounds and Turk had lost 15 pounds; Merrill and I had lost a lot of good sleep. Regardless of all the injuries and difficulties we had experienced — all four of us — we can look back on the many wonderful people we met and friends we made. I feel very wealthy in friends, although my pockets are empty. For what do coffers of gold profit a man if he is without friends?

Also I treasure the memories I'll always have of the Chisholm Trail ride itself — the beauty of the flower-bedecked plains, the clear streams and all God's handiwork. The ribbons of highway were a contrast to the hoof-packed trail we veered off to so many times in trying to follow the exact paths of those of long ago. It was great to rock along in the saddle on this memorable trip as my friends at home rocked in their chairs thinking how foolish I was.

Chapter XI

I AM one of thousands of Americans who hold a high regard for Daniel Boone. He has been somewhat of an idol to me. He was a quiet man, yet a strong leader. He grew up to love the forest just as I have always loved the out-of-doors. At sixteen he was known as the best hunter in Pennsylvania where he was born. The forest was his only school, yet in some way he learned to read and write and master figures; this helped him tremendously in making his surveys later.

In 1769, Boone was captured by the Indians. He hunted buffalo and other wild game with them, but soon escaped back to his own people. He went as far in his travels to what is known as Yellowstone National Park. He became friends with John Coulter, who discovered the park. At first it was called Coulter's Hell. Coulter's friends made fun of his talking about hot and cold water spurting out of the ground. The old frontiersmen kidded him and called him a liar; it was just a big joke to them.

Later when Carson, Bridger, and other explorers went out there they found it was exactly as Coulter had described it. Coulter's wife was a Hooker. I could never find out much about her, only that she was known as the Georgia Corn-cracker. John Coulter lay dying in the cabin where he and his wife lived. A huge Osage Indian friend stayed there and took care of them; he shot game and brought food to their table and protected them. Boone stopped there on his last trip back from the park, to see the Coulters. The Indian stopped him as he approached through the woods and refused to let him pass. Boone told him who he was, but the Indian told him to wait there until he went back to Coulter and verified his identity. Then Boone was allowed to pass and visit his friend that night. Coulter died soon after that; the Indian took Mrs. Coulter back to her people. Recently, someone on an excavation crew dug up Coulter's diary, wrapped securely in oil skins.

As stated before, trails and roads were very important to the expansion of our country. In 1775, Boone and his wood-choppers started from the old block house in Virginia and cut out Boone's Trace. Even so, other hunters had been there before Boone. As early as 1673, Gabriel Arthur emerged as the first white man to travel over what was later known as the Boone Trace and found what was later known as the Cumberland Gap.

Marshal Hooker standing outside his log cabin, built in 1843, with Boone's rifle. Hooker used to make replicas of this rifle in the cabin.

Boone and his trail blazers built a fort called Boonesboro on the Kentucky River. The road ran almost 300 miles through the most bloody and dangerous country in pioneer history. Indians lurked behind rocks, in crevices, and around many turns in the trail. By 1800 more than 200,000 settlers had traversed westward into Kentucky over this difficult and hazardous route.

The Wilderness Road led through rich prairie lands of Kentucky and to the middlewest. Sometimes it was called the Kentucky Road. It began at the block house in Virginia, crossed through the Powell Mountains down into Powell Valley, then it climbed into the Cumberland Mountains, through Cumberland Gap and finally stretched out on the plateau of central Kentucky. It was rocky and very mountainous, a good hiding place for Indians and bandits.

Such a great man as Boone is difficult to emulate, but I had a yen to follow his tracks over the Wilderness Road. I knew it would help me to gain more information about early American history, and I share Boone's love for traveling. I had been a deputy sheriff at Silver Dollar City in Missouri for three years. Silver Dollar City is a tourist attraction and had sprung from the interest in Marvel Cave. As the years went by and the cave's beauty, uniqueness and mysteries were realized, different displays of arts and crafts of the Ozark Hill people were structured around this center of interest. Shops, jail, post office and other businesses were designed with the flavor of the old west days. Shoot-outs in mock battles were staged at certain times; it was an interesting job for me. In the fall of 1963, when the tourist season was over, the Herschends (owners of the city) gave me the opportunity to bring another of my dreams to reality. I left on October 28 to walk the same trace that Daniel Boone and his party had blazed.

I went by Daniel Boone's and his son, Nathan's, farm near Matson, Missouri and drove to the block house in Virginia. After leaving the block house I began my walk over the Cumberland Mountains. I spent a day atop those beautiful hills. It was an inspiration beyond description. Boone had said of the Cumberland Gap, "It is a fearsome and awesome sight." Through the timber I could catch views of the Holsten Valley for miles, although it was misty. I walked Boone's Trace over the gap and down to the old iron works mill, arriving in the town of Cumberland Gap. Just to have the privilege to behold the magnificent beauty of the Cumberlands was most satisfying — a marvelous display of God's handiwork. The Cumberland Gap

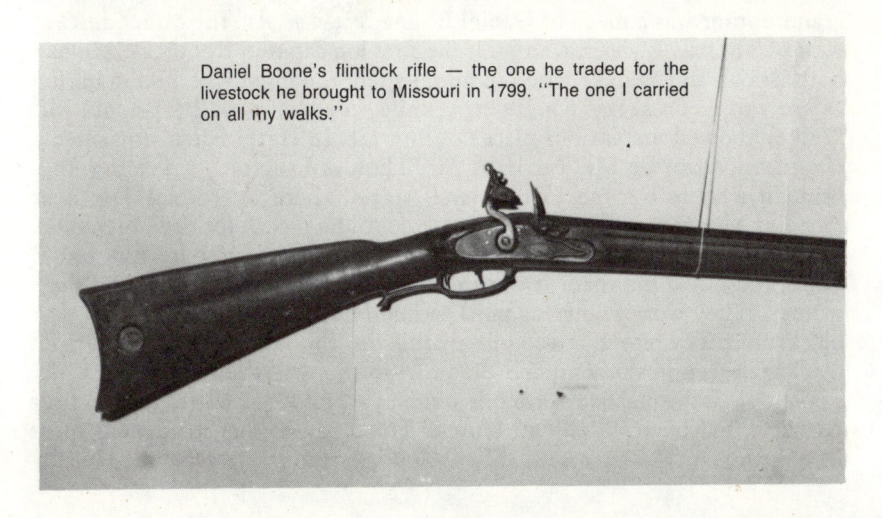

Daniel Boone's flintlock rifle — the one he traded for the livestock he brought to Missouri in 1799. "The one I carried on all my walks."

is a natural pass through the Appalachian Mountains and was used as a gateway to the west by the settlers.

Besides the verdant, luscious, dense growth of the timber and wildflowers the area is covered with breath-taking rhododendrons and laurel in June. The first settlers of Kentucky used the Gap in 1750; it was also used by the Union Armies during the war between the states, when they invaded Tennessee.

Steve Shedd came from Wichita, Kansas to join me in walking part of the trail. We went past the original location of Martin's Station; this was the last outpost going west, where wagons had to be left and the trail had to be either walked or horse-ridden. We visited a large cave which was still littered with human bones. We couldn't tell if they were Indian or white men's bones. We crossed the Indian Creek where, in 1773, Daniel Boone and other families from the Yadkin Valley, North Carolina started the westward journey from the Clinch River. They camped here on Indian Creek for the night. Boone sent his son, James, back to guide the Russell party; James started back with Captain Russell's son and others. They foolishly made camp and spent the night here instead of going on to join Boone again. At dawn a group of Shawnees led by Big Jim, a supposed friend of Boone's, wounded and tortured James Boone's party before killing them. However, two escaped. We stopped at their graves and silently paid tribute to a brave people. Boone's party turned back in sorrow, having lost their desire to continue their trip. This happened just east of Cumberland Gap, close to Gibson's Station which was later established.

When I reached Middleboro, Kentucky the rain sifted through the cloud and drizzled down all day. This is really where the trace started. It was only a trail — not a road — very winding and without any system of planning. It had followed the buffalo trails and sometimes was identified only by marking trees. Traveling into Pineville, I was awed by the beautiful country. It all still looked so primitive with the vast mountains in the distance and the dense foliage of the trees.

I stopped at Hazel Patch to visit with A. J. Walker, whose great-great grandmother was a niece of Daniel Boone. He was also the direct descendant of Thomas Walker, who built the first log cabin in Kentucky. He had both Boone and Walker blood in him. I spent the night with him in his log cabin, and at breakfast I ate with a knife and fork used by Boone. Mr. Walker showed me various places of interest. In Hazel Patch we visited a tavern once run by Mr. Farris. A Mr. Thomas Langford, a wealthy Englishman who had come to buy land, stayed there overnight. The next morning two men and three women came to the tavern for their breakfast. Langford paid for their meals and left with them. Later he was found murdered down the road. It was the crime of the Bloody Harps and their women. They were known as the Terrible Harps; not only were they part black and part white, but also bloody thieves. I took a piece of wood from the locust tree in the yard and drank from the well they had used.

We visited the massacre grounds at the Levi State Park where twenty-four pioneers had been killed and buried. The story of that incident is most interesting: In October of 1786, a band of about thirty people, led by

A. J. Walker holding Daniel Boone's rifle at a house Mr. Walker built. He is a decendant of the Boones and Thomas Walker who built the first log house in Kentucky.

McNitt, Ford, and Barnes and their families and slaves (from Botetourt and Rockbridge Counties in Virginia) were out on the Wilderness Road near Langdon, Kentucky. One woman had a dream three nights straight; they were going to be massacred by Indians. She begged her husband to go back, but he paid no attention to her. On this night at camp the party was drinking and really living it up. Sometime in the night a band of Chickamaugas hit the camp, killed and scalped twenty-one, took five women prisoners, took horses and cattle and some household belongings. Now this woman who had the dream ran in the darkness and stumbled into a huge hollow tree. After the Indians left she gave birth to a baby girl. After a couple of days some white hunters came looking for the delayed party. The woman thought it was the Indians returning and that her time was up! After hearing the men talk, she realized help had come. She was very sick and scared and started screaming and crying. The hunters thought it was an Indian trick to ambush them when they came to investigate. They surrounded the tree with their long rifles ready. The woman was rescued and taken care of, and she and the baby both survived. (Years later, while walking down the streets of a distant town, she came face to face with her husband who had escaped into the darkness. Each had thought the other one was dead.) The slain were found under piled brush and given a decent burial. We camped there by the cemetery, which is walled in and kept mowed and repaired. In the museum at the park are some pewter plates and other articles picked up after the massacre. A marker, "The Last Supper," is also there.

Mr. Walker was my guide; we searched and found much of Boone's Trace, Skagg's Trace, and Harrod's Trace on our way to Harrodburg. We followed the traces as well as we could; the terrain became flatter and less pretty. We passed by Raccoon Springs where Boone had killed so many raccoons, then we parted company at Corbin.

I stopped at Renfro Valley and visited with Mr. Laird, a friend of mine. I slept in the old Opera Barn where Red Foley had his beginning as a western singer. I had an interesting visit with Ole Joe Clark, a forty-two-year old banjo player and singer who had made a few records and broadcasted over

Daniel Boone rifle, bullet pouch and powder horn at bronze marker in old Boonesboro in Kentucky.

the local station. He gave me a number of things to add to my collection of Boone memorabilia.

I continued on through Richmond and into Boonesborough — a trip of 300 miles. When I arrived at Fort Boonesborough, I stood on the banks of the Kentucky River and visualized so many things that had happened at the old Fort. Let me tell you what I did with Boone's rifle here. I read all the time that if you shoot a muzzle loader with the barrel dirty, and the ball does not seat tight on the powder at the breech end of the barrel, it will blow up. Now I know proper loading is right, but what you read by some of these writers of today doesn't always prove true. That day I took some pictures of the Boone rifle leaning against the brass monument there at Boonesborough. Then I thought it would be nice to leave a bullet from the old rifle there. A beautiful hard maple tree was by the marker, so I loaded the rifle up (the barrel was really dirty by now and I had no equipment to clean it out). The ball stopped about a foot from the breech. I thought about all the warnings I had read about shooting with the ball part way down. Now the barrel of Boone's rifle is soft iron and a hammered job. I wanted to shoot it so badly and leave a ball in this old tree where Boone had stood. I took a chance and fired it into the tree. Nothing went wrong, so I loaded it again and put another ball into the tree. Now I know two balls from Boone's old rifle are there at old Boonesborough. I could go back and put my hand right where they are. Don't go trying to shoot with the ball part way down, but that is what I did. And I don't think it hurt the barrel any either, for I have downed buffalo with it since — one shot.

I was privileged to make this trip again when I joined a group of men wanting to walk the trace in honor of the two-hundredth birthday of our country. It's great to be an American and have the heritage of forefathers of strength and untold faith; for a country is only as high in quality as its people.

Chapter XII

MY zest for riding or walking the trails of the forefathers was as much a desire for learning as for adventure. Actually feeling the trail under me gave me a greater satisfaction than all the volumes I ever read about them. To really see the scenic surroundings and imagine the adventures that took place gave me a sense of relationship to the past.

What possesses a man to leave the comforts of his home to sleep on the cold wet ground, endure all kinds of weather, feel the loneliness in the stillness of the night, eat unsavory food in dirty places and encounter other hardships for the sake of reliving a ghostly past? I suppose it's an insatiable desire like those who love antiques, collect coins or old cars must feel. The past is very important to the present as well as to the future. It's the foundation to build the future upon. It takes the nitty-gritty of down-to-earth living to appreciate the present and future goodness of life.

I was given the opportunity to ride the Ozark Frontier Trail in 1966. I started out on May 22, on a 15 year old sorrel mare named Penny, who belonged to Clarence Witt of Carthage, Missouri. We turned south into the Ozark Mountains; the old Ozark Trail extended from St. Louis to Oklahoma City — 600 miles — with little variation on either side as a normal trail. It then fanned out from Oklahoma City to different parts of the country. Markers with O. T. inscribed, designated the original trail. In the early days it was marked with paint on rocks, trees, or anything along the trail. (The Ozark Frontier Trail had nothing to do with the Ozark Trail. The governors of four states — Oklahoma, Kansas, Arkansas, and Missouri — organized this trail by interesting various towns in more tourist trade. This trail was designed to bring recognition and business to the interested areas. It zig-zagged around in a circle of 2558 miles. Sometimes there were feeder roads to towns, perhaps 15 or 20 miles off the trail.) The genuine Ozark Frontier Trail went south to Lawton, Oklahoma, west to Dodge City, Kansas, north to St. Joseph, Missouri, and east to St. Louis. Most of it was over highways which were not very good for horses to travel. Before the trip was over, I had Penny shod twice.

When I reached Bentonville, Arkansas I found some wild strawberries which sufficed for my supper. I slept on the wet ground and practically froze

Marshal Ralph Hooker on Penny starting his 2558 mile Ozark Frontier Trail ride in 1966.

to death. I built a fire and heated some rocks and placed them at my feet to keep warm. From Winslow, Arkansas I entered the Boston Mountains, which are a part of the Ozarks, looking down into the lush green valleys dotted with many cattle. I breathed the invigorating crisp, clean air and felt like singing "How Great Thou Art," but I was afraid I'd scare the wildlife. Close by I saw a clear, pristine stream of water tumbling down off a rocky ledge, having left its cool refreshing spring. These mountains are thickly spotted with springs that bubble out of the earth's fissures.

    I stopped at Van Buren, Arkansas and spent the night in a hotel to get a good bath and get rid of many ticks that had greedily dug themselves into my flesh. In Sallisaw, Oklahoma I visited with friends who were of the real western cowboy breed and who stood up many times to the meanest of killers. The sheriff in this town was E. W. Floyd, brother of Pretty Boy Floyd, the outlaw. South of Muskogee, I crossed the Illinois River where the Cherokee headquarters was located in 1829. Here the tribes gathered and got paid by the government or got their food supplies. The weather was cold and stormy; the creeks were dirty and trash was floating around in careless abandon. I usually rode about 30 miles a day, and could arrange to be in a town at nightfall. Lawton was the farthest south the trail took me. At this time there were race riots in Lawton. Government men, deputies, and police squads swarmed the town. I was wearing my 45 as I approached the city limits; the lawmen asked me not to go into town. I explained to them that I was being paid for visiting all the towns on the trail and couldn't bypass Lawton. They argued that my wearing a gun and riding into town would only stir up more problems. I could understand what a tinder box it was, so I compromised and rode only to the city limits.

As I rode into Tulsa, I entered oil well country. The pumps that pounded into the ground for "liquid gold" looked like huge dark ogres clawing away at the earth. In contrast to this cold, mechanical jungle were the peaceful pecan groves and fields of short buffalo grass in the outlying areas. I crossed Polecat Creek into Kellyville. Al Jennings, a renowned outlaw of years ago, robbed the store in this small settlement several times. One of the bullet holes left by his gun can still be seen in the floor by the door. Near this town a storm came in and steadily got worse; the lightning zig-zagged across the angry sky and the rain fell in torrents. Four days I traveled through this storm, sometimes sleeping in barns, sometimes in deserted houses. Some of the towns were dirty with cans and trash littering the streets. In many of them the people were most unfriendly. In one of these places I was afraid to eat, so I bought a quart of milk feeling it would be safe to drink this for my supper. It was sour! It's a good thing I had jerky in my saddle bags for I had to be satisfied with that for the day.

As I rode north to Apache, Oklahoma the weather began to fair off and become warmer. I camped that night at a beautiful spot on Chandler Creek and stuffed myself with ripe sand plums that grew wild in the area. This was Comanche country, and a young Indian man came to my camp to visit with me. It was a perfect night; I awoke about two o'clock in the morning and the moon was like a beautiful lantern hung in the sky. As I lay on the ground I could hear the bull frogs croaking their serenade down by the creek.

I arose early and continued on my way and camped north of the Washita River. Both Penny and I were very tired. I had lost the canteen I used on my Santa Fe Trail walk in 1958. It was a sentimental piece of equipment for me. I must have dropped it in the high grass some place along the way. I rode 25 miles that day; it was hot and we had to rest often. When I crossed over into a small town I met a bit of excitement. This town was predominantly black, and as I rode out three large fellows came running up to me. One grabbed Penny's bridle and another came for me. I guess they intended to pull me off the horse and rob me. I was wearing my nickle-plated 45 Colt, once carried by Sam Sterling, U.S. Deputy under Hanging Judge Parker. I pulled out this

Marshal Hooker at Guthrie, Oklahoma during his 1966 Ozark Frontier Trail ride.

Colt (No. 92489) and shoved it into one man's face and said, "This gun has killed nine men and it's ready for number ten." I looked him steadily in the eye. About this time Penny got into the act by trying to scalp the fellow holding her bridle; her teeth were in good condition. The men let go and backed off. If the man that tried to grab me hadn't backed off I'd have let him have it, and potted the other one, too, but they got the message and hurried off. I heard one of them say, "I don't want to be number ten." The third fellow had made no move to join them; he just faded into the background.

Many times I made camp for the night, slept awhile, then moved on in the dark. Some folks were so nice to me; they brought me breakfast when they found out where I was camping. They invited me to talk to them about my trip and my gun. When I reached Kingfisher, I visited with two deputies who were very kind to me. They gave me some fried chicken for supper! East of Kingfisher I camped on the cold ground and ate jerky for supper. But there was lots of Johnson grass for Penny. The area was infested with tarantulas, but no rattlesnakes.

Crossing Pawnee Creek into Guthrie, I was met by some of the citizens who wanted autographs and pictures of me. Penny hadn't had any grain for several days and this tended to make her more tired. I set up camp outside of town, caught a few winks and was suddenly awakened by a cold rain. We got saddled up and rode out about 4 o'clock in the morning. By the time we got to Langston, the wind was so violent that Penny could hardly walk.

As I passed over the Cimarron River I stopped and watched it idly flow along, smoothly and peacefully. Yet I had always heard that during a hard rain, this is one of our most dangerous rivers. It goes on a furious rampage, destroying everything in its path. Rain seemed to be my constant companion.

When I reached Perry, Kansas I cut some hay and made a bed in a large culvert near the road. The highway was very busy and I was afraid Penny would wander off in her grazing. I tethered her close by and she seemed to be content. People saw the horse out there in nowhere and would stop in curiosity. When I emerged out of the culvert with my beard, long hair, and pistol strapped on, it really shook them up. Some would peel their tires in getting away.

It always brightened my day when friends from around my home drove up to places where they knew I would arrive, and visit with me for awhile. It's good to see home folks when you've been away. Many were friends I had made on my Santa Fe Trail walk.

By July 3 I reached Kingsley, Kansas. It was 104°, hot and dusty. Penny and I were hungry and tired, but just as we got settled for the night hordes of huge grasshoppers surged around us. They came at us so thickly that Penny was about to break loose and run. The grasshoppers had eaten the ground clean; I saw lots of jackrabbits, but no grass. The next day was the 4th of July, and what a miserable day it was for Penny and me! Carloads of young people would drive by and toss lighted firecrackers under Penny's belly. I finally gave up and made camp early in a wheat field where Penny had lots of good grazing. We broke camp before dawn and reached Pawnee Rock early that morning. This was the place where young Kit Carson (16 years old in 1826) shot his own mule, thinking it was an Indian. The thermometer reached 111° as I wandered on; this cut down our mileage per day! When I reached Ft. Riley I camped on government property. A man and his daughter brought some oats for Penny and some cold lemonade for me — and word that I couldn't stay on this government property, so I left. I suppose I felt that as a taxpayer, I should be able to stay there; I sneaked back to spend the night, but the spiders and ticks were so bad that I couldn't get much sleep.

One night I camped east of Silver Lake, and the mosquitoes were out in full force. With the heat of the night and the bombarding from the mosquitoes, it was another sleepless night. Suddenly Penny had had enough of this and broke loose. I caught her and we moved on.

On the 14th of July, I arrived at Basehorn, Kansas. I tried to call home to Carthage but all the phone lines were out because of an explosion at the Hercules Powder plant back there. For two days those phone lines were out of order.

When I rode into Dodge City, Kansas I looked very much travel worn. My clothes and even my horse showed the dirt and dust of travel. At this time a group of wealthy cattle men brought a large herd of long horn cattle in from Texas. They transported the cattle by trailer trucks. They took the cattle off in old Dodge City. This was going to be the last time herds would be driven through the town. When I rode up I looked authentic in my trail-worn attire and people thought I was the one who had driven the cattle through. The Texas men went into the restaurants and spent lots of money, changed clothes and came out with fancy belts, spurs, and two ivory-handled guns in holsters; they looked like movie cowboys. The people thought these men were just a bunch of dudes, so I was the one who got the attention and requests for pictures and autographs. This made the cattlemen angry and they wouldn't let me ride along with them to the stockyards, but I trudged along behind. I was fascinated by those big longhorn cattle with horns averaging six feet across. Some of those cattle had been raised by hand and were gentle and tame. However some were wild and when anyone came close to them, they'd lower their heads and curl their tails warning everyone that they meant business. The cattlemen had tried to instill fear in the crowd, but I had never had fear for animals and wanted my picture taken with those magnificent beasts. I finally talked a photographer into taking a couple of pictures. He jumped up on the top of a car while I backed up against the herd. The Texans yelled and screamed at me that those cows were dangerous and for me to get out of there. I ignored them and got several good pictures.

After Atchison, Kansas we crossed into Missouri. It felt good; we were on home soil. But I still had a "fur" piece to go. I slept in a pasture where Penny was in grazing paradise. Nevertheless the mosquitoes made life miserable for us, so I saddled up and walked part of the night to fight off our adversaries. The next day I was really tired and hungry. And Penny was beginning to suffer with painful saddle sores. When I came just north of Independence, a friend doctored Penny's back. I discarded one saddle blanket and cut holes in the other to give the sores relief.

While in Independence an incident occurred which truly disgusted me. I went to a cafe for my dinner when a local cop came in and asked if I had any identification. I was taken by surprise and asked him why. He said that a man had broken out of Leavenworth Penitentiary the day before and escaped on horseback. I knew he had to realize I couldn't be that man — this was just a form of harassment. I was wearing a gun and this was a hot bed for gun haters and communism. I have been on TV for days and in the newspapers, all regarding my trip, and the letters OFT designating Ozark Frontier Trails were displayed on the back of my shirt. Yet he claimed he'd never heard of me or my trip. The man who escaped was young, blue eyed, clean shaven, and weighed 175 pounds. How stupid can people get? I showed him my Deputy Sheriff commission from Jasper County and my National Peace Officer's card, but he wouldn't accept anything as proof. He wanted to get me on any charge so he could arrest me for carrying a gun. I became mighty angry, and the people in the cafe began booing the officer. I went to the phone planning to contact the garment manufacturer who was my sponsor for the trip. He had told me before I left on the trip that if there was any trouble at any time, I could depend on him to furnish me with a lawyer. The officer backed off then; I told him to either arrest me or get away from me. By this time my dinner had gotten cold. I mounted Penny and rode off. I was seething inside because there was one man who represented the law and he made such a fool of himself and the law. Some try to act like "Big Shots" because they wear a badge. It makes it difficult for honest people and easy for crooks.

In Washington, Missouri I stopped at the home of Dean Andrea; this was a beautiful mansion built in 1824 by Rogers McClean, the great great grandfather of Mr. Andrea. Dean also owns the Boone house at Matson, Missouri. Old Mr. McClean died at the age of 96. He was the doctor who took care of Daniel Boone as he lay dying. I had a wonderful time visiting that day — only made 20 miles.

The weather was turning colder with a constant falling of rain. The next night I found an empty house to stay in, out of the weather. The following day I camped by the side of the road where Penny enjoyed the good grass. The rain kept falling and I was chilled through. Outside St. Genevieve, I made camp down in a river bottom surrounded by brush and tall grasses. The ground was damp and cold; I built a fire to dry myself. As I prepared to leave the next morning, I heard a car stop on the highway but paid no attention to it. I was busy dousing my fire when I heard approaching footsteps. I turned to see a man coming towards me with a rifle, intent on robbing me. I whipped out my Colt and he changed his mind — in a hurry. I went back to clearing up my camping gear, and rode away on Penny, heading up the hill towards the highway. The road lay along the edge of a bluff, from which the view of a distant valley was breathtaking. I rode past a camper on my way to the very edge of the bluff to take a good look. As I passed the camper, a woman opened the door and called out, "Did you get anything?" Then she looked up and saw whom she was talking to, turned several shades of red, backed into her shell and slammed the door shut.

Marshal Hooker at Boot Hill in Dodge City, Kansas on the Ozark Frontier Trail ride. "I arrived in Dodge City when the last herd of longhorns was brought from Texas."

There's no doubt in my mind that she was a partner to the rascal who came down to my camp. Some way to pay for their travels! I continued for another 25 miles that day. I was stopped by a man who was a horse breeder; he fed Penny and me. He also gave me a New Testament (I guess he thought I needed it). His 16-year-old son wanted to ride a piece with me. About midnight a gulley-washer broke loose and the terrible storm whipped around us. As it eased up, the boy's father came looking for us. The kid decided not to go any farther with me, so his father took him home and I moved on alone.

In Farmington, Penny slipped on wet brick pavement and it caused her to go lame. This, of course, cut down on the mileage, since I couldn't ride her when she was in pain.

When I got to Ellington, Missouri I spent the day being interviewed for TV, radio, and newspapers. This was a restful day for Penny. As I rode down the street leaving town I heard a man say to his friend, "Which one of your brothers is that?" as he pointed to me. That was the wrong thing to say about me that day; I was tired, hungry, and mad. I went towards him and asked, "Is there anything wrong in being a brother to me?" He hung his head and walked off. The people stopped laughing. I guess I was bedraggled looking in my soggy western clothes, but I was might disgusted with the unfriendly attitude. I was glad to ride out of there. After I had ridden a short distance, a car stopped and I recognized the man who had insulted me. I thought he was going to give me trouble, but he walked over and said he just wanted to apologize for being so rude back there in town. "I hope you'll forgive me. I just thought I was smart and funny." I shook hands with him; it took real courage for him to do that. It also helped me to face a better day.

As I rode ahead a thick blanket of fog closed in and the weather was most disagreeable. I couldn't make much headway. We camped off the road and at 3 o'clock in the morning I got up and built a fire and warmed some rocks to keep me warm, but they didn't stay warm without a cover. I planned to cross the Jack's Fork River by ferry but the ferryman refused to take me over with my horse. I would have swum the river but I was already freezing. I asked a woman who was driving her car onto the ferry to send a highway patrolman to the ferry. The ferryman had second thoughts and took Penny and me across without charge. Across the river was Eminence, where we spent the night with a good friend, Mr. Bolin, a deputy sheriff who also owned a restaurant in town. That evening we put on quite a show of rope twirling and trick shooting for the amusement of the customers.

The next morning as I went on my way I came around a bend in the road and saw a group of small cabins. The site was in low bottom ground and was ideal for Penny's grazing. I hoped I could spend the night there. As I rode up to the small grocery store and office, I saw a young woman getting into her car. She spied me, got out and came over to see what I wanted. She seemed very upset. I told her I wanted to spend the night there, and identified myself so she saw I wasn't some hobo off the road. "I'm so glad you came along," she said, smiling and heaving a sigh of relief. "Would you care to stay here all night and watch the place for us?" Then she told me her father had had a heart attack, and she and her family wanted to get to the hospital in Poplar Bluff. They wanted to spend the night at his bedside but had no one

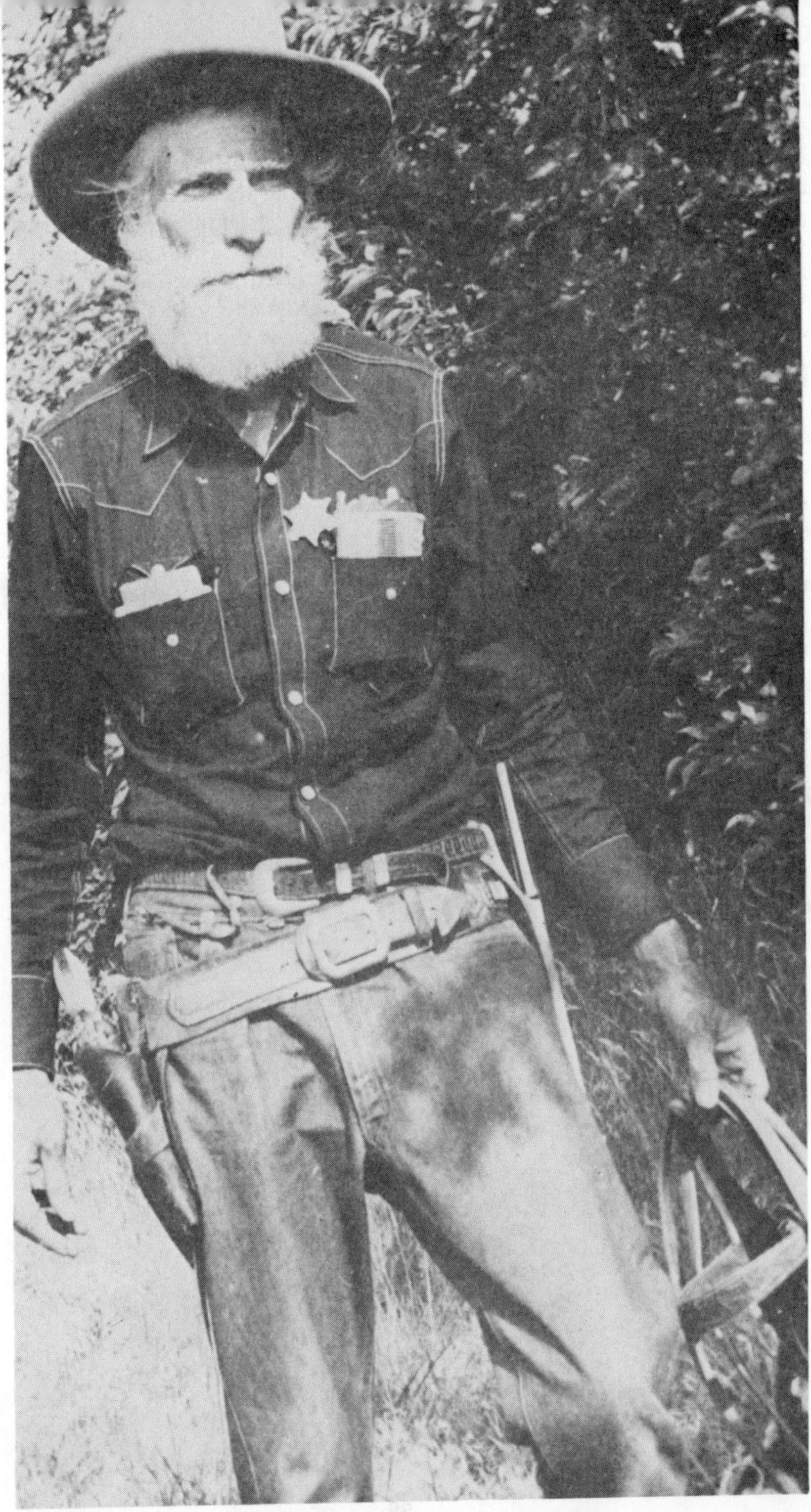

to mind the place. I agreed! — had a good place to sleep, supper and breakfast provided, and a good place for my horse.

The next day I rode 20 miles in the stormy and rainy weather. By evening I reached Viola, Arkansas when another burst of the storm washed through the small town. There were several barns along the street and I asked permission to stay in one for the night. When the saddle and blankets get wet it's hard to ride and also causes galling on the horse's back, but everyone in town refused me shelter. I was dumbfounded at such ill treatment. Wearily and disgustedly I took my horse across the tracks and found a deserted house. I tied Penny outside and entered the dirty broken-down place. I spent the night on a pile of corrugated iron roofing material — not a feather bed — and the roof leaked and kept me soaked all night.

At Cotter, Arkansas I crossed the White River and headed for Flippen. There I bought a grain cradle and carried it to Yellville, where a friend of mine, Glen Hickey, deputy sheriff, shipped it home for me. By the time I reached Omaha, Arkansas the rain had stopped. Penny's back had slowly been healing and we began making better time. I stopped at Branson and at Paul Howard's Confusion Hill, also at Silver Dollar City. From there, Mrs. Fanny Nickels rode to Springfield with me. In Springfield I was on TV, and then rode on toward Carthage and home. Before I could enter my home town I had to stop at Rawhide Territory, six miles south of Carthage. This is a fun spot, a replica of frontier days. I had been marshal there a few years before. I stayed out there for two days while plans were being completed in Carthage for my homecoming celebration. They had to contact various state officials and dignitaries. When they were ready for their parade and other festivities the city officials sent a police escort for me. At last, on July 22, I reach home; this trip had taken 97 days.

It is interesting to note that on this 2558 mile trip there was only one livery stable where I could stable my horse. These shelters are almost a thing of the past. This one was in Oklahoma. It was a nice little ride. I figured I had gone farther on a "Penny" than any other person ever had!

And so, another adventure came to an end, with happy experiences, meeting and making new friends, and seeing more of this beautiful country. But this wasn't the end of my trailing days; there was more to come.

Chapter XIII

IN March of 1775, Daniel Boone and a party of thirty men set off to build the Wilderness Road through the Cumberland Gap into Kentucky. On April 10, 1975, eight of us started from the Yadkin Valley near North Wilksboro, North Carolina to take the same route — my second time. We left from the old Daniel Boone cabin site. Our leader was Ivey Moore of North Wilksboro, who made the trip in the part of Daniel Boone. Ivey Moore was the oldest living Eagle Scout at 72, and was also the 4th great nephew of Daniel, being the great grandson of one of Daniel's brothers. Moore was a retired furniture manufacturer and had spent many years as wagon-master of an annual wagon-train festivity in North Carolina. He was a historian and an authority on the Daniel Boone era; he also had vast experience in walking the trails.

Moore's 14 year old cousin, also named Ivey, portrayed the part of Israel Boone, Daniel's son. Chief Rol Talbull of Springfield, Missouri represented the Indian friends of Boone. He was decked out in his full Indian regalia, complete with colorful head-dress. Chief Talbull was commonly known as Russell Sage Carter, but he has much Indian heritage behind him. He was 77 years old at the time. Like Moore and me, he was well grounded in the history of the pioneer days. His great grandmother was a full blood Cherokee; another grandmother was Chickasaw and was carried as a baby over the Trail of Tears — the migration that occurred when thousands of American Indians were forced out of southeastern United States into Oklahoma, then called Indian Territory. Many died from the hardships of that journey. Russell was born in a tepee on Pawnee Bill's Ranch near Pawnee, Oklahoma, the youngest of eleven children. His great grandmother married old Caleb Carter and they migrated to Green County, Missouri, in 1834 with an ox team. Russell had worked the range most of his life in Colorado, New Mexico, Arizona, and Oklahoma.

George Burks, 28, portrayed George Boone, brother of Daniel. Art Lane, 18, went as Ishmael Lane, an original traveling companion of Boone. Both of these men were from Richmond, Kentucky. Steve Adams and Dwight Miller of North Carolina were much younger than the rest but were hardy and eager to go. I represented John Hart, one of the men who was in

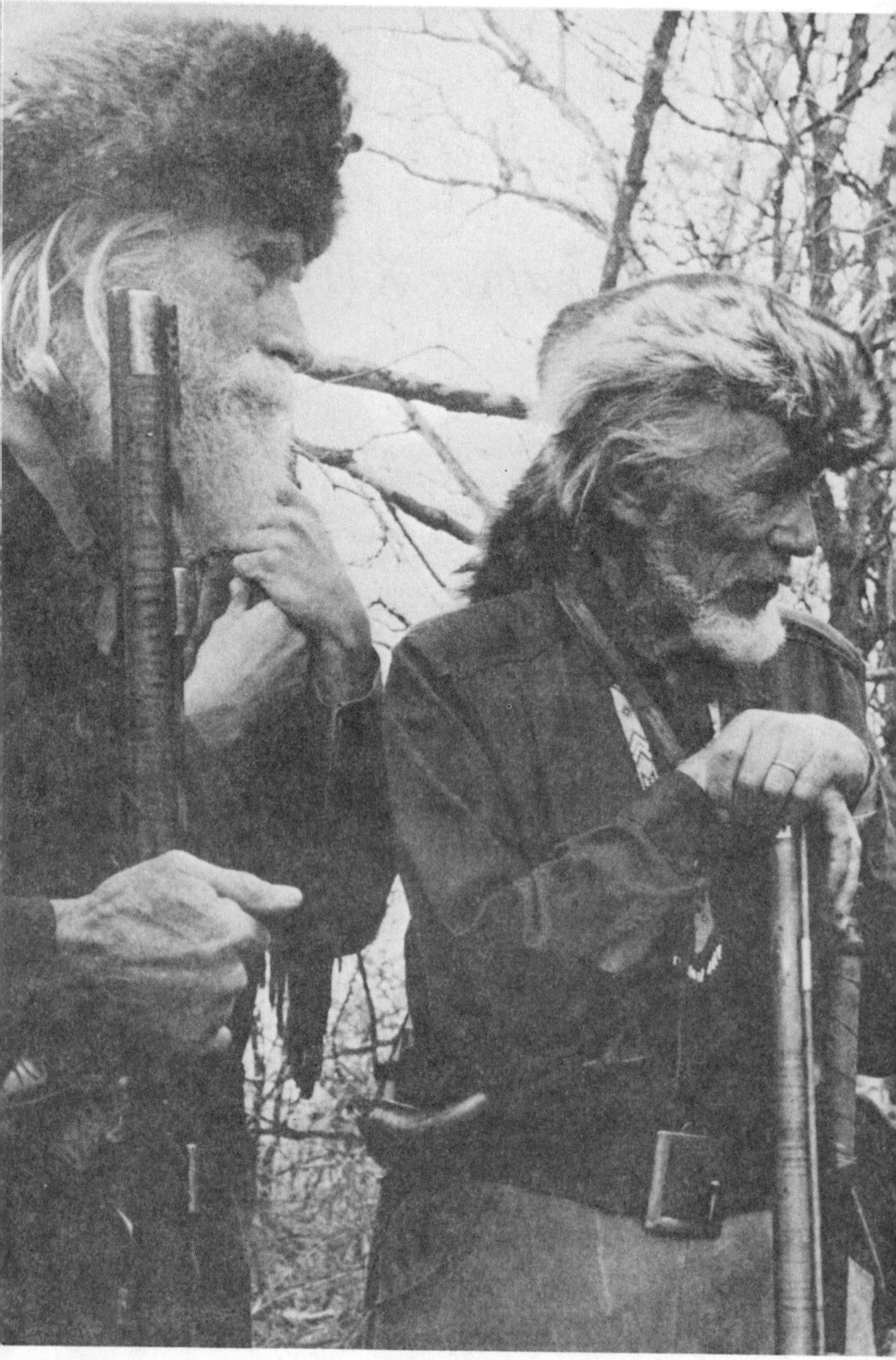

Some of the participants of the Boone Trail walk. Marshal Hooker and Ivey Moore are shown on the left. Moore was the oldest living Eagle Scout at 72 and a great nephew of Daniel Boone. Above: Hooker and Chief Russell Sage Carter at Hooker's log house at Phelps, Missouri. Carter's ancestors, on both sides, came west on the Trail of Tears March.

Boone's party that cut out the Wilderness Road.

This trip was sponsored by the Bicentennial organizations of North Carolina, Tennessee, Virginia, and Kentucky. All of us except the Chief wore the authentic pioneer garb: coonskin caps, bullet pouches, and deerskin clothing. (The Chamber of Commerce of Greenfield, Missouri, where I lived and was curator of the Greenfield Museum, presented me with a beautiful buckskin suit. This was the forest attire like that of Boone's day.)

The Wilderness Road was originally 500 miles long and was a buffalo trail. However, the revised trail which we intended to follow from Ferguson, North Carolina to Fort Boonesborough, Kentucky was 384 miles, following the Boone Trace — "The Doorway to Kentucky." When Daniel Boone first brought his party through the Cumberland Gap 200 years ago, the only ones around to greet them were a few Indians and bears. Their greetings weren't like the welcomes we received from the various Chambers of Commerce. We had a great deal of television and radio coverage. All the folks along the way wanted to do right by Daniel Boone this time.

When we arrived in Boone, North Carolina a big parade had been organized for us. Great festivities filled the snowy air. We had camped four nights in the Yadkin Valley before we started on our trip. A big wind storm blew one tent to bits. By the time we really struck out on the trail the weather had grown cold and nasty. We were more than 3300 feet high and sleeping on the cold ground was real misery.

Location of Daniel Boone's cabin in the Yadkin Valley, North Carolina. Boone left from here on his first trip to Kentucky with John Finley.

We went over the high Jakes Mountains; the road was very crooked but the scenery was marvelous. We left Mountain City and camped at White Top Laurel where the winds were high and exceedingly cold. It began to rain and the mountains were wrapped in a foggy shroud. The weather in those Carolina mountains was bitter cold and the winds were worse than those of western Kansas. It rained or snowed and the hard freezes were common. At times there was no place for us to escape the weather. We spent many nights out in the boondocks. Sometimes people would look for us so they could take pictures and talk to us; some of our supporters drove our cars and met us at certain designated points.

Since walking this trail ten years before, the greatest change I found was

"Everywhere we went we were met by enthusiastic crowds and friendly people. There were many banquets and receptions for us such as the one in Lexington, Kentucky shown above."

the tremendous amount of trash and the volume of cans. People are so foolish to desecrate such a beautiful country. Indians and bears posed no hazards for us, but we found other dangers that Boone didn't have. There were so many dangerous winding roads with heavy truck traffic. The shoulders were so narrow we had to jump out of the way to prevent being struck. Sometimes we camped at school grounds in some communities in order to use the rest rooms and showers. Then we would spend the next day speaking to students or civic groups.

Taylor Valley is in the foothills of Jakes Mountains. Our camping there was a horrible experience. The wind blew constantly and we had a terrible time trying to light a fire and then keep it going; sometimes it seemed futile. Even the young men in our party suffered with the weather. When people get tired and tempers flare it is so easy to get at each other in anger. There was a wild scene one night on this trip that I'll never forget. There had been some disagreement between a couple of the young men and Mr. Moore. On this night things came to a climax. I was standing about fifty feet away watching the boys in their frontier clothes, the fire light on their faces, and thinking how many times scenes like this had taken place in the past. Suddenly I was brought back to reality when one of the boys raised his tomahawk and stood over two of the other boys, yelling a few strong and terrible words. Everyone waited to see what would happen. No one else came close enough to do anything. For several seconds, I expected to see some skulls split, but finally the tomahawk was lowered, and things got deathly quiet for awhile. Because of this incident, two of the boys went back and did not finish the trip to Boonesborough.

Ralph L. Hooker with the Boone rifle on the 1975 trail walk.

We had plenty to eat along the way; there were many banquets and festivities waiting for us when we arrived at different places. There had been few communities for Boone to visit, but we modern-day explorers were well fed. We did a lot of our own cooking when not invited to restaurants or private homes, and ate well even in camp. We walked 15 or 20 miles a day, sometimes 25. Sometimes we were fortunate to camp beside clear streams; there we could wash our dishes, clothes and ourselves, even though the water was very cold.

In Kingsport we visited the block house site where travelers used to wait until families collected in large enough groups to defend themselves against the hazards of the trip. This block house was built by Captain John Anderson in 1772, but was burned down in 1876. Blockhouses were usually built in a square, or oblong, with two or three stories so that the surrounding country could be watched and defended against Indian attacks. Loop holes were cut in the walls through which muskets could be fired. These forts housed 25 to 100 people. In colonial times these blockhouses saved many lives. They were built in the center of the settlement and settlers ran to them for protection in times of danger.

At Abingdon, Virginia we were met by huge crowds. Many pictures were taken and interviews given. We were given rooms at the Cumbo Motel. I had carried my Boone rifle which was always an attraction. In Abingdon I had my picture taken with the rifle in front of the tree carved with "D. Boone killed a bar in 1775." Another was taken in front of the cave where Boone fought the wolves. It was known as Wolf Hills. We camped out in the park and some Boy Scouts came to visit; I lit a fire for them with flint and steel. Let me digress here a moment: it is one thing to build a fire with flint and steel when everything is favorable, quite another thing when conditions are bad. Try doing it when you have only flint and steel, your hands are frozen and everything is wet or snow-covered. Or when you are so cold your hands are frozen and when you bend over to get some material to burn, your frozen condition makes you start shaking. On my trips I have suffered unbelievable hardships from cold, rain, and snow. Sometimes I never did get a fire started and just endured the suffering. Sometimes I was able to start a fire, put hot rocks around me, in whatever sheltered place I could find and make out pretty well. A good way to build a fire is to use — if you can find any — dead bark from a white oak tree, for it makes less smoke and holds fire for a long time. You can sit over a bed of coals between your legs, wrap your blanket around you and sleep warm as toast. Another way is to build a fire and rake the coals into a hollowed out place in the ground, put a few rocks on the coals, put your feet on the rocks, and with your blanket over you sleep warm. I got these ideas from the early settlers — they did it, and I know it works. I was not able to do this some places on the prairie where there was only grass to burn. Sometimes the old hunters would go to a cold cabin to stay; to start a fire they would fire their guns into something that would catch. Other times they would put a peg of wood in the touch hole of the barrel of the rifle and use the flint lock to start a fire. Sometimes the peg wouldn't keep the gun from firing; in the old, old cabins you can see at the left of the fireplace, bullet holes in the logs about a foot from the ground or floor. Shavings from cedar and sumac limbs were both used as tinder — they have much oil in them.

In the Levi State Park in Kentucky, I saw the tallest dogwood trees I have ever seen — some 50 to 60 feet tall. The hills were covered with thousands of blooming dogwoods — it looked like a fairyland! I've heard ministers tell at Easter time that perhaps Christ was hung on a cross made of dogwood. A curse was put on the tree, and that's the reason they never grow large. Well, they do grow large in favorable conditions. One most always sees them growing along fence rows, and they are small just because they are kept grubbed out. They're like sassafras — never allowed to grow tall again. The

Resting after a day's journey in Tennessee on the 1975 walk of Boone's Wilderness Road.

To Oran Scurlock
From
Ralph

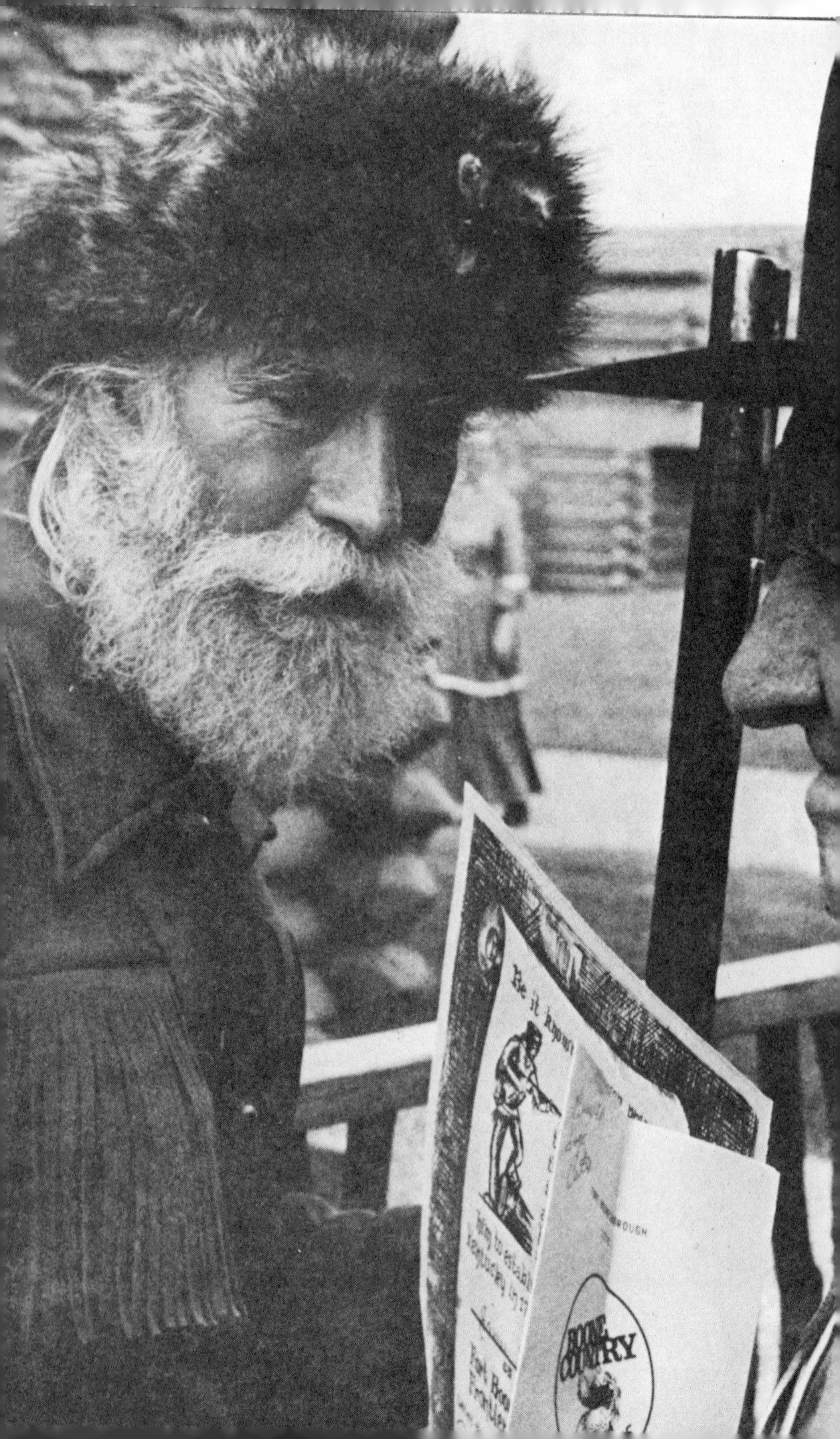
BOONE COUNTRY

"Last Supper" cave is there, too; it's an interesting park. Here again we visited Mr. Laird and the fiddle player, Ralph Marcum.

In Renfro Valley, Kentucky I drank from Boone's spring on the Wilderness Road and took pictures where John Stewart was found dead in a hollow tree. Five years after that, Boone identified his powder horn. Here too, we visited the cave where a negro was hung for molesting a white woman. He was caught and lodged in a log jail. One of the early doctors wanted a human skeleton to hang in his office — the style at that time. So he went to the black man and told him he would give him all the candy, tobacco and fine food he could use if he would give the doctor his body when he was executed. The black man agreed. After he was hung, the doctor was boiling the man's dead body in a large boiler to clean the bones. His sister came out and asked him what he was doing. He stuck a stick in the boiler and lifted up one of the arms out of the water, and the woman fainted! The people who know of it thought it was a real joke on her, and still tell it. When we were there we saw the boiler in the cave — the "Saltpeter Cave." (During the Civil War saltpeter was taken from the cave to make gun powder.)

When we arrived at Fort Boonesborough on May 10, we were met by many dignitaries and the final round of celebrations. Here we bade each other goodbye and turned homeward. It took us 31 days to travel the 368 miles. Governor Carroll made us all Kentucky Colonels. It was an exciting trip over the trail of so much history. The thirst, choking dust, and extremes of heat and cold have always been a great hazard on the trails. They were so in the early days and are still a peril to the modern explorer. Although a great part of this trip was made along the ribbons of highway, still it stirs the heart to know that these modern highways were once Indian trails, cattle trails, and later stage coach roads. They are indeed a heritage of every American, and seem especially ours who walked over it again.

Epilogue

THOUGH I have now lived past three score and ten, I still get the urge to move along some trail, to explore some haunts of bygone adventurers, to meet again old friends of past jaunts. However, as I recall the years of my life, I shudder to think of the escapades of my youth and the foolishness of wasted efforts. This always seems to be the comparison of youthful and mature thinking. My brother, who was a minister, once told me that he wished he had had some of the encounters and pitfalls I had, that his life had been uneventful. I console myself with the thought that although I am ashamed of my conduct and participation in many of those early blunders, it probably was a great help in making me a better lawman. As a peace officer, I many times drew on my knowledge gained by living with outlaws and villains; I knew how they thought, how they schemed, and what motivated them to action.

In these past years I have surrounded myself with replicas of the old west. With help, I built a two story log cabin one mile north of Phelps, Missouri. We built this cabin of hand hewn logs and chinked the cracks with lime. My wife, Katy, and I lived there for several good years. We had electricity but enjoyed the soft glow of kerosene lamps; no water piped in but the bucket of fresh well water and the dipper stood beside the wood burning range. The pot bellied stove in the living room warmed the two rooms downstairs, then radiated the heat through its pipe into the bedroom upstairs on its way out through the roof. It was primitive but cozy. Like our home in town, it was filled with warmth and happiness. Our front door always stands open to receive friends or anyone in need.

I have seen terror in the eyes of a child and fear in many grown-ups' eyes. Despair I have seen often, but the most pitiful of all to me is the sad look on the faces of older people. When one realizes that he or she can no longer do the things they have always done in their lives, and they'll have to depend on and be helped by others, and know it will be like that for whatever time they have left, it really is a SAD thing. Now I am beginning to know just how it is. Even if one has financial security, there are other things needed which someone has to do for us. I would say to you young people, "Don't be ashamed or embarrassed to put your arms around your old father or mother,

Katy Hooker cooks on the wood-burning range in the log home at Phelps, Missouri. The oldest part of this house was built in 1843.

Marshal Hooker in his gun shop at the Greenfield, Missouri museum where he made replicas of Boone's rifle.

or your grandparents, and tell them that you love them." I know how it can make life brighter and easier to bear, and I know how it is to do without it. When you love someone, and they don't seem to be concerned about you or care what happens, it hurts!

Fathers and mothers, be kind to your children; don't find fault with them and put them down all the time. Children, love your parents and try to make them happy and proud of you. So many times we take each other for granted, and when the loved ones are gone we see how a little love and attention could have brightened their lives. This brings me to another thought: I think we should stop and take stock of how we are living as we go along day by day. We know the end of life here on earth is soon coming to all of us, and there are more important things in life than money, fine homes, and fine cars, or enjoying worldly pleasures; let us live what we know!

I can well remember how my good old Christian parents and grandparents left for eternity, each in his or her own way, seemingly looking forward to a better place. And how well do I remember the confusion and despair of some I have known, who had no time for God and a Christian life here, when their times came. How easy it is to let so many things we meet each day — our problems, our work, or whatever — take up our time till all at once we realize there is no more time left.

The apostle Paul said, "If I have hope in this life only, I am of all men the most miserable." For myself, I am satisfied there is a better place for those who have been redeemed from sin by the blood of Christ, and I am determined this is the life for me. What do I care if I am made fun of? Like anyone, I don't appreciate it, but Christ said in St. John 15:20, in speaking of the people, "If they persecuted me they will also persecute you," and another time He said, "The servant is not greater than his Lord." There is one thing that would make it easier for anyone, if this one thing could be stamped in a person's mind, and that is: What God says, He means. There is no way to change that!

Now I know it is not always easy to be a Christian in this old world, and I realize it takes a stronger person to live clean and take what the world does to us, than it takes to just follow the easy way of the multitudes and do what seems the easiest at the time.

I have worked many places, at work that was so hard it seemed each day I could barely make it till night, but employment was hard to come by. So I would go back day after day, and I always kept thinking about Saturday night when I would get paid and have a day of rest. Just so, one can always look forward to a time when we can rest from our labors, in a place God has prepared for those who care enough for Him here to do as He asks us to.

There is an awful responsibility in being a good example to those around us, and raising our children. Parents do a lot of things that they tell their children not to do. But don't be surprised then if they turn out just like you. If you don't want your children to smoke, lie, use bad language, or go places they shouldn't, then don't do it yourself. They can remember how you taught them. People will pull some kind of deal and think they are smart and have gained in some way. Poor ignorant souls! There isn't any wrong you can do to your fellow man that you aren't going to have to pay for.

Marshal Hooker at the 1980 Mid-America Rendezvous.

    The things I have had taken from me, by supposed friends, run into the thousands of dollars. This has hurt me a lot, but when those people come to face God, there will be those things between them and God, and an eternal separation because of greed to have what was not theirs. What a price to pay! It has made me bitter to have these things done to me, and it has taken a lot of time with God to get on top of things. It's not been easy. My first thought has been to get what was mine and to correct the situation. But how can you do this to anyone and not hurt innocent people? It has not been easy to let things go. My son and his wife were murdered, no arrests were made; it was covered up. I had a very rare handgun worth thousands stolen from me, and I put in a claim on the estate of the person who took it — a young punk lawyer sold me out. I have had my own flesh and blood steal from me, and gloat about it. My home was broken up by human beast (again my friends) and I have been betrayed, lied about, made fun of, and put down so many times. I know some of these people would be in their graves today if I were not a Christian. They ought to thank God for that! I do know what is right, even though I have to spend much time seeking strength from God. He gives me strength day by day to manage to overcome the human desire for revenge. He has shown me a better way. I feel sorry for and pity the ones who are so foolish to do these things that will keep them from God forever.

Why is it so easy for people to harm others with impunity and glory in their wrongs?

I have been far from perfect, and so many things I would change if I could; but when I compare my wrongs with some of the things I know about others, I could have been a saint all along. I have never been one who excelled in wisdom, but this one thing I know — God will hold each one of us responsible for things we've done here on earth. How sad to have so much time and so many good things, all from God, and treat Him as if He were unimportant and owed us all this. We should be loving Him and be thankful for all He has been and is to us, and living as He asks — and all for our own good. We know we cannot break even one of God's laws without suffering. Can anyone afford not to live within His laws and love? We may want to live without God, but no one wants to die without Him. And we certainly can't take any of this earth's possessions with us. A life not good enough to die by isn't really good enough to live by, either. And we won't care what friends think of us when we stand before God, so guard your heart and mind at any cost.

I have been at death's door many times, and it is remarkable how quickly the things we cherish here on earth become so unimportant, so empty, so worthless. Friend, take a good look at yourself and remember that there is no way to do wrong and not pay for it. The poorest and saddest person on earth is the one who cannot, or does not, communicate with God. Life is not easy; God never said it would be. We have to trust Him, no matter what.

Here is a poem a dear Christian lady sent to me one time:

"Footprints in the Sand"
One night I had a dream.
I dreamed I was walking along the beach with the Lord
And across the sky flashed scenes from my life.
For each scene I noticed two sets of footprints in the sand.
One belonged to me and the other to the Lord.
When the last scene of my life flashed before us
I noticed that many times along the path of life
There was only one set of footprints in the sand.
I also noticed that it happened at
The very lowest and saddest times in my life.
This really bothered me and I questioned the Lord about it.
Lord, you said that once I decided to follow you
You would walk with me all the way,
But I have noticed that during the most troublesome times in my life
There is only one set of footprints in the sand.
I don't understand why in times when I needed you most
You should leave me.
The Lord replied, My precious child, I love you and I would
Never, never leave you in your time of trial and suffering.
When you saw only one set of footprints
It was when I was carrying you.

AUTHOR UNKNOWN

Ralph L. Hooker and Dennis Weaver during personal appearances at the Coffeyville, Kansas Interstate Fair and Rodeo, August, 1958.

Hooker shot this chicken killing owl through the chest with Daniel Boone's rifle. Below: One of the buffalo he shot with Boone's rifle at Greenfield, Missouri.

For everyone who wants to turn to God: He is longing to help you and forgive you. No matter how sinful or wicked a life, God cares as much for the lowest person and poorest person as He does for the richest and wisest one. He is no respecter of persons; Christ cared enough to die for all. Don't expect this life to be an easy road; prepare for trials, hardships, and disappointments. I haven't put many scriptures in here, but you can get a Bible that has them all! and don't let anyone tell you different. Following the Good Book is the wisest thing you can do. Remember there is only one time around, so don't blow it, or goof it off. Keep in mind that we are not playing games; it's your life after death, too, and you are fixing now how it will be and be forever. I walk the streets in my home town and many times see no one I knew. Nearly all those I was raised with are gone. Everytime I go to a funeral I wonder, "Where are they now?" Of course I have no way of knowing, as no one knows for sure how another person is with God.

Well, in closing, I see a light at the end of the tunnel. Ours is a Christian home; we both try to live and do as we think best before the Lord. We want Him to be first, and when I become discouraged I read and know it will be so for me. Rev. 7:17, "For the lamb which is in the midst of them shall feed them, and shall lead them unto living fountains of water; and God shall wipe away all the tears from their eyes, and there shall be no more death, neither sorrow, nor crying. Neither shall there be any more pain, for the former things have passed away." Matt. 13:43, "Then shall the righteous shine forth as the Son in the kingdom of the Father."

Soon now, I will be leaving this old earth and be seen no more by those who know me. I do hope those who have known me can believe I am with God and my people, enjoying again the life we once had here. I have a lot of things I want to talk about there, and most of all to see Jesus who suffered to redeem me when I was dirty and soiled with sin, and who is the light of that wonderful place. I am not singing the blues and have no complaints. I wish I could do more for my people before I go, and hate to think some of them might need me and I won't be here to help them. But time is short and I feel like the apostle Paul in II Tim. 4:6-8, "For I am now ready to be offered, and the time of my departure is at hand. I have fought a good fight, I have finished my course, I have kept the faith; henceforth there is laid up for me a crown of righteousness, which the Lord, the righteous judge, shall give me at that day; and not to me only, but unto all them that love His appearing."

Friend, if you have to crawl on your hands and knees to get to heaven, it will be worth it. Here we stand to lose everything or gain it all. This is so important; try to realize it. No one can help you at the Judgment. You will be on your own with the record you have made here. After seventy-five years of living, seeing, and experiencing the good and the bad, I know there are many people smarter than I and I feel like giving advice, not of my wisdom, but from God's wisdom. His wisdom brings to every person who follows it life everlasting around the great throne of God in heaven where all is perfection as only God can make it.

As time goes on and I am forgotten, if some soul reads this little book, and only one person gets inspiration to turn from a life of sin, I will at least have one star in my crown, and my efforts will not have been in vain. Try to remember always: any kind of wrong will hurt you; any good will be good

for you, and it is God's way.

    I leave you with this one thought: burn it in your memory until you can't forget it, and make it your way of life. Deut. 6:5, "And thou shall love the Lord thy God with all thine heart, and with all thy soul, and with all thy might!"

The best to you in God
from the old marshal,
Ralph L. Hooker